The de Némethy Years

The de Némethy Years

One Man's Influence on American Riding

Paula Rodenas

ARCO PUBLISHING, INC.
NEW YORK

Published by Arco Publishing, Inc.
215 Park Avenue South, New York, N.Y. 10003

Copyright © 1983 by Paula Rodenas

All rights reserved. No part of this book may be reproduced, by any means, without permission in writing from the publisher, except by a reviewer who wishes to quote brief excerpts in connection with a review in a magazine or newspaper.

Library of Congress Cataloging in Publication Data

Rodenas, Paula.
  The de Némethy years.

  Includes index.
  1. De Némethy, Bertalan. 2. Horsemanship—United States. 3. Horsemen and horsewomen—United States—Biography. I. Title.
SF284.52.D4R6   1983   798.2′092′4 [B]   83-11798
ISBN 0-668-05678-9

Printed in the United States of America

10 9 8 7 6 5 4 3 2 1

Contents

	Preface	vii
	Foreword	ix
1	*"A Legend in His Time"*	1
2	*The Early Years*	27
3	*Show Jumping and the USET*	37
4	*At Home and Abroad*	55
5	*The Olympics and the Pan American Games*	77
6	*De Némethy on Course Design*	95
7	*The de Némethy Touch in America*	111

8 *Looking Ahead* 127

*Appendix—Major USET Jumping
Victories 1956–1980* 143

Index 191

Preface

For twenty-five years Bertalan de Némethy successfully coached the United States Equestrian Team jumpers, and today, following his so-called retirement, he continues to exert a tremendous influence on the sport of show jumping. Although I had long been an admirer, I did not have an opportunity to become acquainted with Bert until 1981, when I interviewed him for a magazine article. While many articles had been written about him, especially after his official retirement, it occurred to me that a man of his stature deserved a book.

I put aside the idea of a biography in favor of an assessment of the man and his influence on riding in the United States because, in some ways, Bertalan de Némethy would not be an easy subject. His perfectionism and modesty would have to be overlooked, and his privacy could not be invaded. There are many areas of his life which he does not wish to share. It is also difficult to separate the man from the Team; volumes could be written about the United States Equestrian Team and its members.

It is my hope that I have met the challenge of dealing with de Némethy's influence and of combining the events of past and present in the world of show jumping to highlight his role and contributions.

Because it was impossible to speak to everyone who had worked with de Némethy—or even to mention all the names—I had to content myself with the observations of a few individuals who had known him over a long period of time. Bert's busy schedule allowed for little free time, yet he made himself available to me for discussion as often as he could.

I would like to extend my thanks to all who lent their support, especially the United States Equestrian Team.

PAULA RODENAS

Foreword

I am delighted to have been asked to write an introduction to this book about Bertalan de Némethy, a truly remarkable man with whom I have been associated, as horseman and friend, for more than three decades. When I first met him, Bert had only recently immigrated to the United States; he knew hardly anyone, his command of English was limited, and memories of the cavalry troop he had commanded on the Russian front were still fresh in his mind. Today, in comparison, he is nationally recognized as one of the most influential figures in equestrian sport in the post-war era, a man whose teachings, both directly and through his many pupils, have exerted a profound influence on the success of our international team and the general standard of equitation in the United States, and indeed, Europe as well.

How did all this come about? It is too simplistic merely to assert that Bert was the right man at the right time in the right place, though he was surely that, as well. Perhaps the developments of the "Némethy Era" will be easier to under-

THE DE NÉMETHY YEARS

stand if we first briefly review the historical context into which he projected himself, some thirty-odd years ago.

First of all, it is important to remember that most American equestrianism (Western riding excepted) was based on English models right from the Victorian era through the 1920s. Our general style of fox-hunting, polo, hunt racing, coaching, horse shows—all had been imported more or less intact from the country of our mother tongue, along with generations of English and Irish trainers, instructors, and grooms to show us how to do them properly. True, there were always a few isolated "voices in the wilderness" attempting to teach us such fancy Continental things as dressage and the Italian forward seat, but it was not until Los Angeles hosted the Olympic Games of 1932 that the horse community became generally aware that a lot of the world played equestrian sport quite differently than we did at home. And this situation in turn depended in large measure on the fact that most official international equestrian competition was strictly limited to cavalry officers and the occasional artilleryman. (At the Berlin Olympics in 1936, for example, there was only a single lonely civilian, Dutch three-day rider Eddy Kahn, among all the uniforms.)

During the years before World War II while our officers were practicing over European-type obstacles at Fort Riley and using international (FEI) scoring, American show jumpers for the most part were still jumping traditional English jumper courses of rails, walls, gates, and the odd triple bar or hogsback, and competing mostly with touches to count. I must say that the best riders of that era were highly accomplished horsemen, many still in the English style—foot "home" in the stirrup, the leg rather straight, the toe just slightly down. However, while they rode with great accuracy and made a fine art out of "sharpening up" horses to jump big verticals without ever laying a toe to them, their methods were often very personal and idiosyncratic. Indeed, there was a general tendency to think that every horse had its own special "key"—some particular bitting arrangement or schooling

FOREWORD

procedure—and unless you got the "key" when you bought the horse, you wouldn't be able to reproduce its best form.

By the 1950s the really traditional English seat was rapidly disappearing from the show ring, and the forward seat (which had been the subject of bitter controversy only twenty years earlier) had become dominant, thanks to the teaching and writings of such horsemen as Harry Chamberlin, Piero Santini, Vladimir Littauer, and Gordon Wright. Nonetheless, few of us who were showing jumpers at that time knew much about Olympic-type courses, or international rules, or how to prepare our horses or ourselves to cope with them. Since the Army was responsible for all our international equestrian representation there was not really much need to, and it was not until our horse cavalry was mechanized after the 1948 Olympics, and we had to put together a "civilian" team to go to Helsinki in 1952, that we started to address ourselves in earnest to the task of learning how to play the European forms of the equestrian game. We found that we had an awful lot to learn.

The new civilian U.S. Equestrian Team was just starting to think about the 1956 Olympic Games when young Captain de Némethy, not yet ten years out of the Army, found his way to our shores. A member of the Hungarian squad for the ill-fated 1940 Olympics, Bert knew all about the European horse-show scene, and from what I have learned of it subsequently, the contrast with what we were doing must have come as quite a shock to him. Be that as it may, there can never have been a doubt in his mind that he had a real contribution to make to us, whether in riding, training or course-building. In place of our random "keys" he could substitute a soundly progressive basic methodology, evolved from the teachings of the Cavalry schools of Hungary and Germany, filtered through Bert's own keen intelligence and sensitivity, and gradually adapted to the particular needs and temperaments of American riders and their (for the most part) Thoroughbred horses. And in place of our old-fashioned courses—Pat Smythe termed them "prehistoric" when she jumped at New York in 1953—Bert could invent truly fascinating challenges to horsemanship and intellect, courses that conveyed at the same time some sense of Bert's own aesthetic and highly imaginative phantasy.

Only a fortnight ago as I write I had the pleasure of witnessing, in the lovely old Imperial city of Vienna, the 1983 FEI World Cup Finals. Numerically the European riders predominated in the field, but at the end the winner was an American who, like three of the four previous finals winners, had passed considerable time under de Némethy's keen and thoughtful scrutiny. "Oh, how I wish our riders would copy you Americans," a European journalist exclaimed afterwards. "You not only win, you ride *beautifully*—not all just the same, of course, but all working towards the same ideals."

And in the final analysis, it is probably this idealism about equestrian sport that is the most important part of the legacy Bert has brought to his adopted home. For nobody has better manifested the conviction that if you are going to participate in equestrian sport, you should take it seriously, and bring to it the very best qualities you possess—the highest intelligence, dedication, unselfishness, courage and even taste that you can muster—to go with whatever talent and mechanical skills you were born with or can develop. It seems to me that Bert's career has exemplified the most demanding connotations of three very demanding designations: officer, gentleman, and horseman. (I was tempted to add a fourth, Hungarian, but Bert is legally my countryman now.) Perhaps I can sum it all up best by saying that few of us who have come under his influence, and had the experience of working with him towards a common goal, and knowing him as a friend, can ever forget our debt.

WILLIAM STEINKRAUS

1

"A Legend in His Time"

A handsome silver tray in the home of Bertalan de Némethy commemorates his official retirement as United States Equestrian Team (USET) show jumping coach after twenty-five years, during which time his influence was felt far beyond the circle of the Team. The tray bears the signatures of 45 members of the U.S. Jumping Team, as well as this inscription:

TO
BERTALAN DE NÉMETHY
USET JUMPING COACH 1955–1980
WITH GRATITUDE AND APPRECIATION
FROM YOUR TEAM MEMBERS

But "retirement" is scarcely more than a word in the dictionary to Bertalan de Némethy, who continues to follow a schedule that would exhaust many a younger man. He acts as a consultant to the USET and fulfills certain obligations: conducting training sessions on the East and West coasts for selected riders; serving on the selection and jumping committees sharing in the discussion of Team activities with William Steinkraus, Frank Chapot, George Morris, Chrystine Jones, and other representatives; attending designated Grand Prix competitions, including those at Tampa, Florida;

THE DE NÉMETHY YEARS

William Steinkraus, former President of the USET, presents silver tray (*below*) to Bertalan de Némethy to commemorate his "retirement." *Courtesy of Bertalan de Némethy*

Charlotte, North Carolina; Valley Forge, Pennsylvania; and Newport, Rhode Island, to observe and select riders; and serving as chef d'equipe for the National Horse Show in 1981 and 1982 and for the World Championships in Dublin in 1982. In addition, he rides Team horses daily as his schedule permits, judges and officiates at prestigious shows and clinics, and virtually circles the globe in a tireless effort to contribute to the sport he loves.

In January 1982 he was appointed by the FEI (Fédération Equestre Internationale) to conduct a judges' clinic in Australia, with sessions held in Sydney and Melbourne. He judged at the Lucerne CHI (Concours Hippique International) in May 1982 and at Hickstead, England, one week later and ten days prior to the World Championships. The final selection of four out of six riders for the World Championship Team rested with him—an awesome responsibility for anyone, at any age. In recent years he has become a much sought-after course designer and lecturer. He was asked to reproduce the plans for his World Cup course in Baltimore in 1982 for a European seminar, which he viewed not merely with personal satisfaction, but as an excellent opportunity to show the Europeans what is being done in the United States. He is designing the Olympic course for 1984 in Los Angeles and eagerly accepts the challenge as a chance to prove that America is right up there with the best! He also hopes to prove that he is "not too tough a course designer." It is little wonder that, on many occasions, Bertalan de Némethy has been called "a legend in his time."

CLINICS

De Némethy has conducted instructors' seminars and limited private clinics, preferring to work with small groups of no more than six horses and riders. It is through his teaching that his unique qualities become evident. His understanding of human and equine psychology is clearly visible. "You resist certain people," he observes, "because they cannot do any better than you and because they put you down and never build you up. It is very important to explain and criticize only what you know you can change and are able to demonstrate. You must have discipline, or you lose your influence."

These words reflect the cavalry training of de Némethy's youth. Remembering the officers who were his instructors, he explains, "We did our best to please the instructors who were not arrogant." This memory carries over into his own instructing, where he is always the gentleman, inspiring respect and the desire to please. He jokes about teachers who shout angrily to terrified students, "Relax!" and then expect to get good results from the fear they instill in the riders.

De Némethy's enthusiasm is infectious. A touch of humor in his instruction sparks interest and ambition and avoids the "factory work" monotony of riding.

"Riding has to be enjoyable and interesting," says de Némethy. "It is not a contest of strength between a horse and a human. The point of riding is to understand the animal and conquer him mentally and physically, so that he follows your commands, and to develop an 'equestrian language' through signals."

Warmth, quick wit, and keen intelligence are distinctive of de Némethy's personality and are mirrored in his teaching. When the horses and riders are performing well, he will raise the fences, gleefully calling out in his Hungarian-accented English, "Higher and vider!" Of a horse that trips going through the *cavalletti*, he philosophizes, "He will be more careful next time." A commonsense approach, with emphasis on the basics, leads horses and riders through the initial work on the flat that prepares them for jumping. Positions are analyzed, corrections made, and the horses ridden in both directions at all movements until they are flexible and moving forward freely and rhythmically. De Némethy is careful to make the schooling sessions interesting for the horse and not too repetitious.

The tone of de Némethy's voice communicates a lot to riders going over fences; it becomes stronger to indicate that something more is needed and quiet when all is going well.

Getting over the fence is not in itself important, he explains, but *how* you do it matters greatly. The horse must be balanced, moving in the proper rhythm (which has been established through work on the flat and over cavalletti), and not "diving" over the obstacle. The rider is cautioned to refrain from "chasing" the horse over or anticipating the jump. He is told to "feel" the striding, even as the fences are raised or widened, and relaxation is emphasized (though not by shouting!).

"Don't be like a little tin soldier," de Némethy directs. "Riding should be like the ballet." The rider develops the proper feeling through time, practice, and the right kind of exercise, which is necessary for all athletes. The horse, too, is prepared by the work over cavalletti and gymnastic jumps, so that he will eventually be able to jump bigger fences without losing his frame, rhythm, and confidence. The use of cavalletti will lead to learning to "feel" the take-off point—the most desirable point from which to jump—which varies according to the type of jump. The take-off point of an oxer, for example, will differ from that of a wall or a water jump. It is the most sensitive moment for the horse, de Némethy explains, a moment in which he must be coordinated, concentrating, and making an effort. If the rider disturbs the horse in that tenth of a second, he cautions, he risks losing the horse's confidence, which, in turn, can lead to refusals and runouts. Too often he has found that riders resort to "gadgets" as the problem gets worse rather than look to themselves for the cause.

Gymnastic jumps are actually a continuation of the cavalletti. De Némethy ingeniously uses the right combinations to teach the horse to lengthen and shorten without losing his natural balance, as well as to help the rider perfect his timing. It is important to consider the horse's conformation, says de Némethy, illustrating that the average American Thoroughbred may have difficulty with short distances, while some other breeds may not be as handy at lengthening. One must also consider the horse's ability and level of training.

Balance is all-important. While some riders are more naturally balanced than others, de Némethy believes that practice can result in improvement. The instinct of both horse and rider, he explains, is to regain their balance when they lose it. Speed changes the horse's center of gravity, so the rider has to train himself to follow it as the horse moves, turns, and changes his speed, always trying to be at the right place on the horse in relation to the center of gravity, and as close as possible to the body of his horse.

"The relationship between horse and rider exists through the reins," de Némethy tells his riders, urging them not to "hang" on the horse's mouth. It is important, he emphasizes, not to disturb the horse's balance in any way—for example, by anticipating the jump and getting ahead of the horse or by interfering with the landing.

In the best tradition of his former cavalry training, de Némethy is always ready to illustrate a point. He will put a young horse on the lunge line to relax him and obtain further understanding and obedience. He makes it look easy, but lungeing, as employed by de Némethy, is an art that must be done correctly, until the horse accepts the bit and the signals of the unmounted rider or trainer. It can take days or weeks to get the desired response, he warns, depending upon the horse's disposition. Training should never be hurried.

On horseback, de Némethy demonstrates clear application of aids and the use of the seat to influence the horse. He cautions against confusing the horse with conflicting signals, such as a contradictory use of rein and legs together: the animal does not understand whether to go forward or decrease his impulsion. On one occasion, European dressage instructor Maria Gunther was watching him ride, marveling at his skill and remarking that his methods were exactly in keeping with the classical principles. "He is the best in the world," she declared.

"You can stay on top longer in riding than in most other sports," de Némethy has said, but he adds that it also takes longer to learn. Developing an independent seat and learning to stay with the center of gravity are primary rider goals; practice and repetition will help to obtain the right "feeling," which cannot be fully explained by an instructor, nor can it be developed in only a few sessions.

A recent photograph of Bertalan de Némethy on horseback, explaining some principles at a Stonyhill clinic. *Courtesy of Edward Felumero*

Elementary training (that is, elementary dressage) teaches the horse balance at all gaits before jumping is introduced. Cavalletti teaches him to concentrate, and gymnastic work enables him to lengthen and shorten his stride while maintaining his natural balance and rhythm. "The aim of training," de Némethy concludes, "is to have a pleasant, relaxed, obedient horse."

De Némethy finds that too many people tend to complicate

the art of riding, which began in the sixteenth century and developed according to classical principles which have remained virtually unchanged to this day. A good example is the Spanish Riding School of Vienna, whose traditions have been handed down through the centuries in an unbroken line, unaffected by new ideas or fads. De Némethy is critical of some of the modern practices that detract from the purity of the concepts—for example, rushing of the training of a horse, which should be done slowly, carefully, and systematically. He feels that the popular "crest release" idea that is seen today in equitation competition is not practical over higher fences; the rider's arms should follow the motion of the horse in an unbroken line, being in easy elastic contact. In the crest release, the rider slides his hands along the crest, which lessens the chances of disturbing the horse's mouth and offers more support to the upper body of the rider. He compares the action of the rider's arms to that of rubber bands. De Némethy is outspoken against the use of artificial practices in riding, for example, such gadgetry as tight martingales, and, where juniors are concerned, cautions that equitation classes should not present the problems of Grand Prix jumping.

The building of the rider's confidence is important to de Némethy as a teacher. "It doesn't matter if you are an Olympic rider or a fourteen-year-old student," he says. "You have to build up your confidence and ego." He urges instructors to "be generous with praise" and emphasizes the need for plenty of hours of practice. He compares riding to flying, in which a pilot must log a great deal of time and experience or risk a crash.

Clinics, de Némethy believes, can be helpful to a rider and regenerate interest. Selective reading, he adds, can also reveal answers to questions.

"Riding is actually very simple," he has often been heard to say. "Nothing has changed in riding in many hundreds of years. The horse's construction has not been 'rearranged' and probably will not be in our lifetime." Some might point out that the forward-riding style championed by Federico Caprilli was an innovation, but, even there, the rider follows the motion of the horse and remains balanced over his center of gravity, adapting his position to the action of the horse (jumping).

At the end of one of his recent clinics, de Némethy repeated the old Steinbrecht quotation: "Make your horse straight and ride him forward." Twenty-five years ago, the statement might have had little impact, but today it rings true and can be understood, thanks to de Némethy's own example.

De Némethy has conducted clinics in many parts of the United States and Canada, as well as in Venezuela, England, Poland, Switzerland, and other countries. Raul de Leon, a noted Long Island instructor who has been organizing clinics since 1965 and describes himself as a "de Némethy watcher" of many years, states: "For any serious student, an opportunity to ride with de Némethy should not be missed." He praises the logical sequence of de Némethy's system, pointing out that his knowledge comes from many sources, including the best classical cavalry training available before World War II, personal observation of the Italian methods at Passo Corese, one of the former facilities of the Italian cavalry, and study at the Hanover Cavalry School of Germany with some of the world's finest teachers. De Némethy blends the perfect balance precepts of classical riding with the modern Federico Caprilli technique of following the motion of the horse and exposes riders to gymnastic exercises that challenge them beyond their expectations.

While some may proclaim de Némethy a miracle worker, a solemn word of advice to those who would ride with him is that they must do their homework. To get the most out of the master's class, the students should already have a pretty good understanding of riding on the bit, extension and collection, lateral work, and the use of cavalletti. It is also important that the riders believe in the system and continue to follow it, not merely give it "lip service."

A RIDER'S VIEW

Regina Anne (Gina) Morin has been studying and practicing the art of teaching and training horses for approximately twenty years. Her show record proved her to be a good rider, and she was respected by her peers.

When she first became interested in classical horsemanship, or dressage, Gina found some surprises in store. "It wasn't until I became interested in classical dressage that I realized I couldn't ride at all!" she says now. Her past teachers were more involved with working on the "picture" than in concentrating on the function and specific needs of the horse.

Beginning instruction with Raul de Leon, Gina realized that she had no back, seat, or legs whatsoever. "I was so conditioned to using the forward seat," she remembers, "that it was almost impossible for me to sit comfortably on the vertical."

She has no regrets about the strong sense of self-discipline and highly developed eye and reflexes acquired during her early years, but, to Gina, dressage was the "missing link" in her career as a horsewoman.

Gina learned about the horse's anatomy and why it is so important for the horse to be engaged and on the bit. She learned how to turn a horse and get impulsion by activating her calves and not crossing reins on the horse's neck to make him turn. She felt what it was like to get a horse "in front of my leg and have his back come up underneath me, enabling maximum elasticity and freedom of movement." When she applied this flat work to jumping, she had phenomenal results. Much time was spent teaching the horse to relate to cavalletti and gymnastic work. By studying classical dressage, Gina knew that what she was doing and feeling was correct. "It was almost as if I were born again!" she says. But when she went to shows and watched the equitation classes, she saw horses with inverted backs and bad head carriages. Many unorthodox training techniques were being applied in the schooling ring. Since some of the riders appeared to be successful despite this, it made her question and wonder.

She then had the pleasure of participating in several clinics at Stonyhill conducted by Bertalan de Némethy. All her questions and doubts disappeared. "Here is a man the entire equestrian world greatly admires and respects," she says. "He has worked with every top rider this country has produced in the last years. The tremendous success of our Team was nurtured and developed by this man. He is the best we have."

De Némethy spoke a language in the clinics that was totally and unquestionably native to all the classical dressage training which Gina had been working on in the last few years. Studying with him proved to be one of the most rewarding experiences of her career.

As Gina tells it, "It was important to spend much time in suppling both my horse and myself. It was wonderful to see and experience the results of the close parallel between classical dressage and jumping. De Némethy's acute sense and eye for a horse told me, in many instances, of specific problems my horse had, mainly due to stiffness or lack of engagement, which could be improved by suppling him and activating his hind legs. His uncanny method of cavalletti training, in which he demonstrated many flawless exercises, was wonderful. His discussion and practical application of distances and rhythm created a well balanced, receptive, comfortable, confident, and consistent horse, regardless of the height of the fences.

"I trusted Mr. de Némethy completely," she continues, "which enabled me to execute the movements necessary to have complete unison between horse and rider. I knew there was no chance of him overfacing me or my horse."

With the horse so well balanced and trusting, it was easy for Gina to feel comfortable and capable, even when the most difficult tests were required of her.

The clinics confirmed many things for Gina: that a horse must be completely in balance and supple and submissive to the rider's hands, seat, legs, and aids; that good attitude is as important to a horse as talent, because not all horses are equal in their abilities; that lateral movements at all gaits—yielding, shoulder-in, half passes—are absolutely vital in getting the most out of the horse and equipping him to meet the most extensive, difficult demands the rider might place on him; that, to make him more comfortable, the horse must understand a correct half halt, be ridden from back to front, and be alert to his rider and submissive to his hands.

De Némethy told Gina that she must work very hard at training and schooling her horse while adhering to the classical position, staying close to the horse's center of gravity at all times and keeping a balanced seat in all phases of training. It is primarily with "green" horses, she finds, that riders' positions tend to break down. In making allowances for an inexperienced horse, the rider often forgets about himself.

Gina says she is grateful for the opportunities of working with de Némethy and hopes to be able to do so again. Meanwhile, she continues to ride, train and teach, applying the knowledge gained from the de Némethy clinics. Gina is a serious young rider—a thinking rider—whose experience serves her both actively and as an observer. Perhaps we should heed her when she says, "In this day and age, where dressage and equitation are slowly—and sometimes painfully—joining together as one, I hope everyone can reflect on the meaningful accomplishments of all our Team members and take a much closer look at what it took to make it all come true under Mr. Bertalan de Némethy's enlightened heart and hand."

THE DE NÉMETHY DIFFERENCE

In relating the principles of classical dressage to jumping, Bertalan de Némethy differs from those who advocate forward riding techniques. While such horsemen as Gordon Wright, Harry D. Chamberlin, and Vladimir S. Littauer have undoubtedly been successful with their methods, de Némethy's goes beyond. All use the basic exercises of schooling and talk about the horse being on the bit; the main difference lies in the rider's position and the way in which he influences the horse.

Harry D. Chamberlin, in *Riding and Schooling Horses* (Armored Cavalry Press, 1947), cautions against too much collection as being detrimental to the horse, an opinion that is shared by Vladimir S. Littauer (*Schooling Your Horse*, Arco, 1972). Both advise the application of a simpler method to keep the rider in harmony with the horse by means of a forward balance. The rider controls the horse while in this position without disturbing his natural balance and forward momentum. Assuming that the horse travels with most of his weight on the forehand, this position is one of noninterference. Littauer uses the word "engagement" to denote the movement of the hind legs (separately) under the body of the horse rather than in connection with collection.

Following the de Némethy method, the rider is in more of a vertical balance, yet he remains in harmony with the horse both on the flat and over fences. Engagement of the hindquarters means that the horse is using them to propel himself and obtain impulsion, much in the manner of a car with rear-engine drive. As de Némethy explains in Chapter 7, collection has advantages for the jumper in helping him to be able to change his stride to meet the challenges of the course. The ability to execute a pirouette-like turn also makes him handier at negotiating tricky courses. To do so, he must respond to the rider "from back to front" rather than with all of his weight on the forehand. This concept has its roots in the traditions of classical dressage, which many people, unfortunately, look upon as something specialized and mystical. Yet this kind of training benefits not only the horse that is viewed as a future Grand Prix dressage prospect, but also can improve almost any horse. The rider, too, benefits from learning these basic principles, gaining an independent seat that is in balance with the horse's center of gravity and reinforcing it by means of cavalletti and gymnastic jumping exercises so that he does not interfere, but has a positive effect.

The pros and cons of the various theories could be argued endlessly, and certainly all have their merits. A young novice rider might find the subtleties of the de Némethy way difficult to understand at first, while a more simplified approach gives him the coordination and confidence he needs to go further. At the highest level, such as that of international competition, horse and rider must refine themselves accordingly. In this, de Némethy's horses and riders have demonstrated their success over the past two and a half decades.

In a sense, dressage is to riding what ballet is to dancing. In fact, Haute Ecole dressage has often been likened to ballet. While a jumper does not have to reach a point where he can imitate the high collection demanded of the piaffer and passage, he nevertheless begins his education similarly to the horse that will later achieve that level, learning to lengthen and collect and to be balanced, supple, and obedient to the aids. Both are started with the same initial aim: to make them as good as they can be.

Knowing this, one might conclude that Bertalan de Némethy has combined jumping, as a sport, with classical horsemanship, as an art, so that the latter assists the former in a practical way. This, and his use of cavalletti and gymnastic jumping exercises, is what sets him apart from others and makes his method unique.

A typical de Némethy clinic starts with the riders working on the flat, analyzing their positions and striving to get their horses supple, obedient, and on the bit. At the posting trot, the proper frame and rhythm are established, which the riders will try to maintain as they go on to work over cavalletti and jumps.

When de Némethy is satisfied with their appearance on the flat, they begin trotting through cavalletti, a series of poles about 6 to 8 feet long and 6 to 8 inches in diameter, which are spaced evenly on the ground at a distance that accommodates the horses that are using them. Eventually, a low jump is placed at the end of the cavalletti. This can be raised or widened, but the horse's approach does not vary; he continues to trot through the cavalletti without speeding up or changing his attitude in any way.

Later, additional jumps are added to the gymnastic series. Infinite variations of striding can be used according to the needs of the horses, to encourage them to collect or lengthen. Meanwhile, the riders are urged to remain in balance whether the horses are trotting, cantering, turning, or jumping—

always keeping the steady rhythm. Even when the jumps are raised, the horses that have been properly prepared will not become excited or make any noticeable changes in their approach.

Lungeing demonstrations supplement the clinic, as de Némethy demonstrates how it is used to calm a nervous horse, to help the horse find his balance, and to help the rider facilitate the process of getting the horse to accept the bit and the aids. Draw reins or side reins are used to give the horse contact (the horse is always lunged under tack, never in a halter only). Done correctly, lungeing lays the foundation for mounted work by making the horse relaxed, balanced, accepting of the aids, and understanding of the rider's signals. While the Team riders were often lunged in a dressage seat, without stirrups, as an exercise prior to competition, this is usually not part of the clinics.

De Némethy often concludes his clinics with an informal lecture to reinforce what he has taught during the day and then answers questions. His lectures invariably underline his respect for classical horsemanship and serve as a reminder that in riding, as an old saying goes, there is nothing new under the sun.

A LOVE OF THE SPORT

Bertalan de Némethy has been fortunate. In his lifetime he has been able to see the effects of his influence. Few people have actually changed the world, but, in the world of riding, at least, de Némethy has left his mark.

De Némethy's love of the sport derives, in part, from its essential fairness. Unlike some sports, such as dressage, diving, or gymnastics, show jumping is not subject to opinion, but is cut and dry. Anyone can tell if a rail has been knocked down! Furthermore, the results of a mistake are seldom as serious as in three-day, for instance, since the fences are planned to come down easily and the course designer has supposedly foreseen every contingency. Three-day compe-

THE DE NÉMETHY YEARS

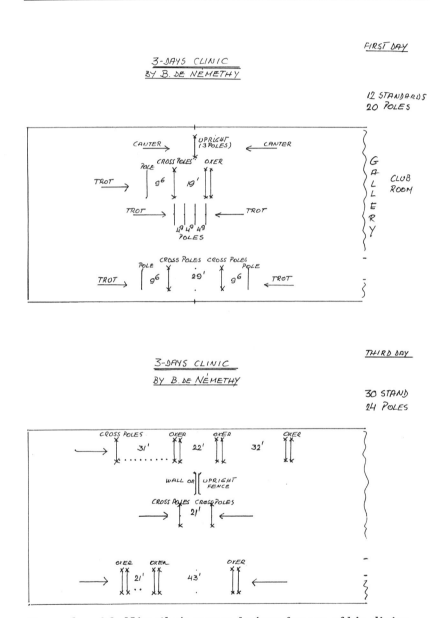

Examples of de Némethy's course designs for one of his clinics.

tition is easier for the rider, in some ways, de Némethy says, because there are several distinct phases and thus several opportunities to excel. Cross-country accidents, however, are usually more disastrous.

The inherent nature of show jumping, he finds, allows for a greater feeling of sportsmanship which is often lacking in other sports where opinion can determine the results. All of his Team riders, he claims—including the women—had discipline and team spirit and did not gossip among themselves. "This is the character of the sport," he says. "The rules are clear, there is no need to gossip."

While the toughness of the male three-day rider may give him an advantage over his female counterparts, the female members of the show jumping team are, in de Némethy's estimation, fine performers. Prior to 1956, women were not allowed to jump at the Olympics (England's Pat Smythe was the first), but because there were so few female competitors, it was not practical to keep them separated, and they were finally permitted to compete on equal terms with the men. "The girls showed they could be not only equal, but better!" comments de Némethy, pointing out that Mary Mairs won a gold medal at the 1963 Pan Am Games over twenty-one male competitors. In dressage, de Némethy believes that women have certain advantages; he finds the female riders light and elegant and less forceful. But in show jumping, too, women have excelled, as exemplified by the performances at the Olympic Games and elsewhere of such riders as Mary Mairs, Kathy Kusner, Melanie Smith, and Katie Monahan.

Married since 1965, de Némethy met his wife, Emily Myles, when she invited him to judge at a Westchester Pony Club show. She knew of him only by reputation, and their meeting turned out to be, in her words, "a lucky stroke of fate." Today they live quietly in a town that is nestled in such a peaceful setting that it almost denies its proximity to the hustle and bustle of New York City. It is a perfect place for "retirement," de Némethy style.

THE DE NÉMETHY YEARS

Kathy Kusner and Nirvana, Lucerne, 1972. "The girls showed they could be not only equal, but better!" declared de Némethy. *Courtesy of the USET*

"A LEGEND IN HIS TIME"

At home, Bertalan de Némethy enjoys a quiet moment. *Photograph by the author*

Bertalan de Némethy in retirement does not fit the traditional description of a senior citizen. His appearance is deceptively youthful; he rides and jogs, takes an interest in current events and the state of the world, exudes warmth and integrity, and is quick to enjoy a good laugh. His blue eyes twinkle to indicate amusement. While his manner is decidedly that of the European gentleman and reminiscent of an earlier era, Bert de Némethy is anything but outdated. With him there is no generation gap. People of all ages respond to his charisma, and he works his magic with riders as expertly as he does with horses. Active and alert, both physically and mentally, he appears to be ageless.

THE DE NÉMETHY YEARS

De Némethy continues to view show jumping from the perspective of the roles he has played: rider, coach, chef d'equipe, course designer, and observer. And although he has seen many improvements over the years, he reminds us that the picture is constantly changing, that we cannot take success for granted—nor should we expect it. "The American attitude," he says, "is that if you don't win, you are no good. Our years of success have spoiled us. You can't always win, because the situation changes." As an example, he cites the two Olympic gold medals won by France's Pierre d'Oriola in 1952 and in 1964, after which the French "disappeared" for awhile, starting to win again only a couple of years ago. The Swiss, likewise, were hardly considered competition until recent years, and now they are, as de Némethy puts it, "right behind us."

A moment of relaxation at the American Gold Cup, 1982, as Bert de Némethy and Bill Steinkraus admire Michael Matz's daughter. *Courtesy Eastern Horse World/Bill Bohn*

When the Americans placed fourth at the 1982 World Championships in Dublin behind France, Germany, and Great Britain, de Némethy was unfazed. "Individuals and teams change," he repeats. "Today we do not have as many experienced horses as we did in the past." He also mentions that faults were incurred in the first round. Had it happened in the second, he points out, we might have had the silver or the bronze. "The horses were tired, not only from the trip, but from the whole season," he explains. Part of the problem with contemporary show jumping is that there are so many shows and such big fences, as demanded by the generous money prizes that are offered today, that the horses burn themselves out in frequent competition. In a way, the progress of the sport has also been its downfall.

The ideal Olympic jumper, says de Némethy, should be a superior Intermediate horse of about eight years that has been systematically and carefully prepared. It is doubtful that such an animal will be available for the next Olympics, as the present competitive system does not encourage such slow, methodical preparation.

The changes that de Némethy has observed over the past quarter of a century have been both positive and negative. The United States certainly cannot overlook its successes: the many Nations Cup victories, Steinkraus's Olympic gold at Mexico City, and the close run for the team gold at Munich. So although Americans face new problems in today's world of show jumping, we should not become discouraged, but should seek answers and continue to train our horses and riders as systematically and carefully as we did during the years in which de Némethy was coach.

Far from being merely a "living legend," de Némethy is still in a position to inspire and advise. His presence on the scene as course designer and chef d'equipe and behind the scene as teacher continues to exert a strong influence and to benefit the sport.

THE DE NÉMETHY YEARS

Bertalan de Némethy today. *Photograph by the author*

CLINIC COURSES

The diagrams on page 18 show clinic courses used by de Némethy at the Stonyhill Farm and School of Riding. The first day, cavalletti rails in the center start off the exercises, which go on to include gymnastic combinations to be trotted or cantered over as indicated. The course for the third or final day consists of different combinations, with many spreads, to be taken at the canter: 21 or 22 feet equals one stride, 31 or 32 feet equals two strides, and 43 feet equals three strides. The horses are collected, ridden deep into the corners, turned very smoothly, and kept at a steady rhythm. Note that the obstacles can be taken from either direction.

2

The Early Years

Bertalan de Némethy was born in Gyor, Hungary, on February 24, 1911. His father governed three of that country's nineteen states. De Némethy was raised in the governor's mansion and educated by Benedictine monks.

The boy's strict academic life was offset by vacations with his grandmother, who had a pony for him to ride. Almost everyone was involved with horses in those years, including his father, who was fond of driving. The early days spent with the pony started an interest in riding, and young Bert was taken under the wing of an uncle on his mother's side who was an officer in the cavalry and who allowed his nephew to ride his horses. De Némethy's uncle was a pretty fair rider who competed in horse shows. He introduced him to his first taste of show jumping at the age of sixteen or seventeen. "That was my start," says de Némethy.

In Europe, in those days, young people were expected to know what careers they wished to pursue upon graduation from the *gymnasium* (the equivalent of our high school). "By that time," explains de Némethy, "you had already decided whether you were going to be a doctor, go to law school, or be a scientist or engineer—or a career officer." The enthusiasm for riding that had been fostered by his uncle led the young de Némethy to choose the military academy of Ludovica, which was Hungary's version of West Point. He had to undergo very rigid physical and theoretical entrance examinations.

At first, de Némethy's father was not pleased with his son's choice. He was the only son, with two sisters, and his father wanted him to "use his brain" rather than become a soldier. He tried to discourage the young man by warning him about the long waits for promotions and the lack of stimulation in such a career, pointing out the benefits offered by other professions. The seriousness of his son's ambition finally won him over, however, and he gave his support. De Némethy spent four years at the Ludovica Academy in Budapest, graduating in 1932 as a lieutenant in the cavalry. His education, he points out, included such academic subjects as mathematics, geography, physics, history, and veterinary studies at the university level, in addition to sports and riding.

Upon graduation, he was assigned to a regiment, the 3rd Hussars of the Count of Nadassy in Sopron, where, for three years, he performed his duties as a young officer. He was one of a half dozen officers selected to be assigned to the Hungarian cavalry school in Oerkeny Tabor.

It was a tenet of the Hungarian cavalry that only the most talented and successful officer-teachers should become riding instructors in the cavalry regiments. They were given an intensified program of instruction by older, highly educated officer-teachers until they were able to earn the respect of the other officers in the regiments they would later be instructing. In Germany, France, Italy, and other parts of Europe, similar systems prevailed.

After the first year, the class was divided, and only the top students were kept on. The officers rode six horses a day, starting on dressage horses, riding on the lunge line without stirrups, later going cross-country on young horses, and, in general, following a progressive, systematic routine.

"The horses and instructors changed, but we were the same!" chuckles de Némethy, remembering the big turnover of mounts and instructors to whom he was exposed. "Today," he laments, "there is no such way—I shall call it 'classical'—for anybody to be sent to learn, because it doesn't exist any more.

There are no specially educated teachers to observe. I rode hundreds and hundreds of horses for two years, riding many hours without stirrups and working with many different instructors. Today there is no one with so much experience on a horse."

De Némethy graduated in 1937 as an army riding instructor. Because of his classification, he was asked to remain and teach. He also became a member of the Nations Cup team of four riders that trained for the 1940 Olympics. The other members included two older officers: Captain Joszef Plattny, bronze medalist in jumping at Berlin in 1936, and Captain A. d'Endrody, who was fifth in the three-day competition at Berlin. The fourth member was Captain Charles Valko, also known in the United States. The Games had to be canceled because of the outbreak of World War II.

FROM GERMANY TO DENMARK

The cavalry was riding Hungarian-bred horses that had a predominance of Arabian blood, but it also had Thoroughbreds, which are still being bred today in Hungary. De Némethy's experience with the Thoroughbred did not begin when he came to the United States, but was acquired in his native country, where he competed successfully on two fine members of the breed. He points out that Plattny also rode a Hungarian Thoroughbred, while d'Andrody, who was small of stature, competed on a small, government-bred horse of mixed bloodlines, which he rode at Berlin. Unlike many of the other European countries, Hungary did not import Irish horses, but supplied its cavalry with horses of good quality that were bred either privately or by the government.

Observation was considered an important part of the army learning experience, and, periodically, two or three officers were sent to other countries, such as Italy, France, or Poland, for experience. De Némethy was the first Hungarian officer to be sent to Germany. The German cavalry school of Hanover was located at that time at Krampnitz, about forty

THE DE NÉMETHY YEARS

De Némethy receives the Gold Cup from Mussolini in 1940 following a Prize of Nations victory with fellow team members, *left to right*, Capt. J. Plattny, 1936 Bronze medalist in jumping at Berlin Olympics; Capt. A. d'Endrody, author of *Give Your Horse a Chance* and 5th place rider in three-day at Berlin Olympics; Capt. Charles Valko, steeplechasing champion and instructor-trainer who died in 1981; and a young Lt. Bert de Némethy. *Courtesy of Mrs. Bobbie Valko, with special thanks to Capt. Andrew B. de Szinay*

miles west of Berlin, near Potsdam. De Némethy had classes with such notable horsemen of the era as Fritz Stecken, Bubbi Gunther, and Otto Lörke, who was a civilian instructor and in charge of the dressage stable. He also competed against many other important figures of the horse world, such as Hans Heinrich Brinckmann, who later designed the jumping courses at Munich and Aachen; Colonel Hally Homm, Kurt Hasse and Ernst Hasse of Germany; Colonel Tommaso Lequio, Colonel Conforti, and Captain Gutierrez of Italy; Captain Fresson and Captain Xavier Bizard of France; Mylius and Mettler of Switzerland; and Colonel Corby, Ahern, John Lewis, and Ged O'Dwyer of Ireland.

De Némethy was expected not only to ride and observe, but also to make reports to the Hungarian secretary of defense about the German system. In future years, Germany liked to claim the lion's share of the credit for de Némethy's success. In reality, however, his basic education began and developed in his native land, and his experience in Germany was the "icing on the cake."

Two months before war broke out between Germany and Poland, the Hungarian military attaché in Berlin informed de Némethy that he would have to return home with his horses, which he accomplished in an arduous journey. Later, in 1944, he was put in charge of the cavalry cadets at the military academy—young men between the ages of seventeen and nineteen—who got out of Hungary just before the Russians closed in on Budapest. Hoping to continue their education elsewhere, they left Budapest only a few days before the city was completely encircled by the Russian army. Keeping ahead of the Russians was only part of the problem; the main concern was finding enough to eat. De Némethy's ingenuity was tested at every step.

In an effort to avoid the Russians, de Némethy moved toward Denmark with his group of cadets. Whenever he was stopped by the Germans, he boldly produced his Hungarian papers, which they could not read, and kept on going.

Ten days later his group reached Denmark, where they were treated kindly and given food and medical attention.

During the next six months, de Némethy assisted the Red Cross in finding places for the young men—sending them to work on farms and getting them settled. Many of them stayed in Denmark, married, and raised families.

De Némethy decided to remain in Copenhagen, intending to look up two old friends who might help him in his career. Sadly, he discovered that one had died and the other was living in Paris. "It was quite a blow," he remembers. Nevertheless, he managed to start out on his own as a freelance instructor, bicycling from place to place to give lessons and gradually building up a following. He taught riding in Copenhagen for six years.

The Danes had been helping foreigners relocate to other countries. When questioned about relocation, de Némethy mentioned the possibility of going to the United States. In reality, however, he was happy in Denmark, where he had learned the language, had made friends, and was making a living that enabled him to help his mother back in Hungary.

ON TO AMERICA

It came as a shock when de Némethy finally received a letter from the U.S. Embassy granting him permission to enter the United States. He had only three weeks in which to decide. As his mother had recently died (his father died in 1940), he no longer had a reason to remain in Europe, close to Hungary. Hearing of the opportunities offered in the United States, and realizing that he had a year in which to make the move permanent, he bid farewell to his students and friends and left Denmark. At the end of a year, he reasoned, he could always return if he wanted to.

But de Némethy did not look back. He arrived in the United States in 1952 and became a citizen in 1958. He began to teach, train, and ride and to make the acquaintance of people who would later play an important part in his life—people such as Arthur McCashin and William Steinkraus, members of the American bronze medal team at Helsinki in

THE EARLY YEARS

One of the earliest known photographs of de Némethy in the United States, taken on Long Island in 1959. *Courtesy of Bertalan de Némethy*

1952, and Gary Smith, the most famous professional rider in the United States at that time. De Némethy recalls weekends spent with Steinkraus during their bachelor days, when Steinkraus worked in New York City and had limited time in which to practice his riding.

One of the first people to help de Némethy in the beginning was General Alexander Rodzianko, who was living in Far Hills, New Jersey. De Némethy paid him a visit shortly after he arrived and eventually wound up settling in the area.

De Némethy taught at the Sleepy Hollow Country Club in Tarrytown, New York, for several years. The enthusiasm of such friends as McCashin and Steinkraus, relayed to Whitney Stone and the USET, eventually led to de Némethy's appointment as jumping coach. Before accepting, however, he had to be persuaded to leave his excellent job as trainer for the noted sportswoman Eleanora Sears in Massachusetts, where he was working with his friend Gabor Foltenyi. His employer was understandably reluctant to let him go. He offered his assistance in designing courses during the winter of 1954–55, but it was not until after the Pan American Games in Mexico City that he agreed to take on the responsibilities of the fledgling Team.

De Némethy's military background and education had prepared him well for riding and teaching and acting as chef d'equipe. There was no question of his suitability for the position he was being offered. Even though the USET was a civilian rather than a military organization, the new challenge appeared to be tailor-made to his qualifications. Working for a private individual like Miss Sears was limiting, he realized, albeit enjoyable, and in his usual fashion, de Némethy chose to look ahead. The USET offered a future and a chance to put his knowledge to work in a new and interesting way.

In a sense, de Némethy was fulfilling his destiny. Had he taken his father's advice and become a lawyer or a banker, his career would have ended with the war. Instead, although his life was taking a new twist, it would enable him to do the kind of work for which he had been prepared. Unlike so many others who had to start anew in a strange land, de Némethy was fortunate in being able to apply his years of study and training rather than lose them.

De Némethy's decision to join the USET was, to him, a logical progression in the course of events. It was a turning point for both him and the USET, and, in keeping with his philosophy, de Némethy did not look back.

3

Show Jumping and The USET

The sport of show jumping began in Europe long before it became popular in the United States. In its early years, it took a back seat to harness competition, and jumping was mainly associated with the cavalry.

Explaining European equestrian history, Bertalan de Némethy reminds us that horses were originally used for agriculture—heavy, strong horses that could pull weight and work all day on the farms. In time, wealthy people began to take an interest in racing and breeding horses for sport and speed.

The cavalry's need was for transportation, and their horses had to be small, easy to keep, sturdy (with an infusion of Arabian blood), physically strong, and systematically trained for military purposes. Larger horses were still needed to pull heavy artillery. Hungary and Germany were the countries most deeply involved in breeding and exporting cavalry horses.

When riding became a sport rather than merely a means of transportation, England, France, and Ireland started to breed and export horses to the United States. The cavalry and three-day riding, particularly the cross-country phase, had a definite influence on show jumping. Three-day was originally a military competition, as good, fast horses were the only means of sending important messages from place to place, often across difficult terrain and over different kinds of obstacles. Cross-country horses had to be very fit, sound, and strong.

What we now know as show jumping was a specialized activity that evolved out of three-day riding. Three-day horses had to be good jumpers, and, in the process of improving this skill, jumping became a goal unto itself.

NATIONAL DIFFERENCES

Serious competition in Europe got under way in the early part of the twentieth century, although no formal rules existed until the British Show Jumping Association was formed in 1921 by a group of cavalry officers. This brought about an improvement in the quality of competition and an increase of interest among civilian riders and spectators. National differences emerged; for example, in Great Britain, speed was not as important a factor as it was on the Continent during the 1930's. Course design became a major consideration in Europe; obstacles were varied, distances between fences were measured to coincide with the horse's striding rather than left to chance, and subtle changes of direction were included.

Americans were not traveling extensively in Europe and were for the most part unaware of equestrian happenings abroad. Jumping in the United States was primarily thought of as an activity connected with fox hunting. In 1883, however, the National Horse Show offered a high jumping contest that was won by a 6 foot leap, and this competition became a standard part of the show. Horses continued to jump higher each year, eventually reaching 7 feet 1 inch, until a new rule in 1892 imposed a limit of 6 feet 6 inches. Cross entries in hunter and jumper classes were quite common. Today the *Puissance* (meaning "strength") class is a reminder of the high jumping competition of yesteryear. Only two obstacles remain for the jump-offs; each is gradually raised, and time is never the deciding factor.

SHOW JUMPING AND THE USET

The Puissance wall has become a traditional challenge of the National Horse Show, recalling the high jumping competitions of yesteryear. Shown here is a member of the Irish team.
Courtesy of the National Horse Show

THE DE NÉMETHY YEARS

America did not enter the European show scene until the 1920's. The United States was represented at the Olympics in jumping during the twenties and missed winning a bronze medal in 1936 in Berlin, placing fourth. The military continued to dominate the sport.

International jumping at the National Horse Show in New York was initiated by Alfred Gwynne Vanderbilt, president of the show, in the first decade of the twentieth century. He recognized the need to introduce something new and exciting and thus proposed to the board of directors the idea of inviting foreign riders to come and compete against American riders. In 1909 a group of British cavalry officers accepted the challenge, and a year later, teams from France and The Netherlands joined the competition. By 1911, international jumping had become an established tradition of the National and was accorded the status of Military Team Competition Division. The outbreak of World War I canceled the National Horse Show in 1914, and it was not until 1925 that foreign teams once again began to appear to challenge the American military riders. Before 1940, teams from many distant parts of the globe had taken up the gauntlet, and the arrival of the Canadian team was looked forward to as an annual event. The rules and scoring system had become far more sophisticated than in the days of the early high-jumping competition, when competitors were simply allowed three attempts to clear each height. When touch rules were introduced, differences in riding styles and in the types of horses entered were noticed, as opposed to those who competed under the knock-down rules of the Continent. Show jumping rules were precisely outlined and carefully observed, and the sport enjoyed popularity as part of the American horse show scene.

International jumping today is governed by the rules of the FEI (Fédération Equestre Internationale) and, in this country, by the AHSA (American Horse Shows Association).

Prior to the formation of the USET, teams for show jumping, dressage, and three-day were fielded by the military. After World War II, the large cavalry centers at Fort Riley and Fort Sill were mechanized, and the need for horses became obsolete. This created a vacuum to be filled, on a civilian level, by the foundation of a new organization devoted to continuing the traditions begun by the military.

THE USET

Following the 1948 Olympics, there was a great void in American equestrian society when there was no longer an Army team to compete at the 1949 National Horse Show. This void inspired the initial steps taken to form the International Equestrian Competition Corporation (IECC), forerunner of the USET. The first meeting was attended by generals Albert Stackpole and Alfred G. Tuckerman, Drew Montgomery, Amory Haskell, Alvin Untermyer, and J. Spencer Weed, among others. Weed was elected chairman of the board, and the president was Colonel John Wofford, who was succeeded by Whitney Stone a few years later. Many retired officers were among the founders of the IECC. Fund raising and financial matters were the main topics of discussion in preparation for getting teams together for the fall circuits and for the 1952 Olympics in Helsinki. The IECC eventually became the United States Equestrian Team, created in 1950 as a nonprofit civilian organization whose purpose was to pick up where the military had left off in supplying American teams for the three major international equestrian disciplines: show jumping, dressage, and three-day.

The charter of the USET restricted its activities to amateurs. "We kept our amateur status," says de Némethy. In other countries, athletes were supported or subsidized by the government, but this was contrary to American policy. Furthermore, the organization was nonprofit and therefore subject to the scrutiny of the Internal Revenue Service. Whitney Stone and the others wanted to be very careful and correct in all legal matters, and for that reason they stuck to amateurs.

THE DE NÉMETHY YEARS

In later years, when professional horsemen such as Rodney Jenkins joined the Team, it was, curiously, not a reversal of the original concept. The owners of the horses accepted the prizes and paid the expenses, and all precautions were taken not to violate any legalities.

When the cavalry disbanded and the question arose as to who would support the international teams, a special consideration was the fact that there were so many kinds of equestrian competition in the United States—many different breeds and riding interests. How could show jumping, three-day, and dressage be promoted without offending the exhibitors of gaited horses, Tennessee Walkers, Western horses, and members of the numerous other divisions that comprise the American horse shows system? The new organization and its leaders agreed to assume both the moral and the financial responsibilities and to provide teams for Olympic and other *international* competition—namely, show jumping, three-day, and dressage—and through good planning, careful legal advice, and capable leadership, this goal was achieved.

The first evaluations of potential Team candidates were held at Secor Farms in White Plains, New York, in the spring of 1950. The first permanent location of the Team was the Alvin Untermyer estate on Taconic Road in Greenwich, Connecticut (1955–1961), but the Team trained several times at Tryon, North Carolina; Avon, New York; Boulder Brook in Westchester County, New York; the Fairfield Club in Connecticut; and the Ox Ridge Hunt Club in Darien, Connecticut.

The USET found a permanent base at Hamilton Farm in Gladstone, New Jersey, in 1960. The farm was part of the late James Cox Brady's estate; the Bradys eventually approved the use of the property for USET headquarters, and the Team moved in upon its return from the Rome Olympics.

The stable at Hamilton Farm was built in 1910, with stalls on two levels. An indoor arena was constructed, outdoor rings carefully graded and improved, and cross-country obstacles provided for the eventers. Today the upstairs trophy room overflows with ribbons that line the walls in glass cases, and impressive silver trophies are displayed around the immense room.

After the three-day team moved to South Hamilton, Massachusetts, the Gladstone center was mainly occupied by jumpers and dressage horses. In recent years there has been a change in the function of the Gladstone facility. It is no longer exclusively a training center, but rather a place for making final preparations before international competitions. Clinics and competitions are held for the various disciplines, but, as John H. (Jack) Fritz, assistant secretary-treasurer

In the trophy room at Gladstone, NJ, Bertalan de Némethy pauses beside one of the numerous prizes won by the USET jumping team. *Photograph by the author*

of the USET, has commented, "The USET is no longer producing, but finding horses and riders."

OLYMPIC DEBUT

The new United States Equestrian Team made its debut at the Olympics in 1952. The FEI had voted against allowing women to compete in jumping at the Olympic Games, although Carol Durand had been selected as a Team member. The American team that finally competed at Helsinki consisted of William Steinkraus, Arthur McCashin, and John Russell, with Norman Brinker as the reserve rider. They had surprisingly good success in pre-Olympic competition in Europe, winning at Dusseldorf, and Russell became the first foreign rider to win the Hamburg Derby. In 1955 an American team competed for the first time in Europe during a non-Olympic year (at London, Dublin, Rotterdam, and Le Zoute, Belgium).

In those days, there were only three riders, and all three scores counted in the Olympic competition. At Helsinki, the Prize of Nations was, for the first time, a two-round event. The United States took the team bronze behind Great Britain and Chile, and since the three-day riders also won a bronze, things were looking up for American equestrians. It was the first time that an American team had ever won a team medal in Olympic jumping, which gave a big boost to the morale of the American riders and their fans.

In 1954 Bertalan de Némethy and Gabor Foltenyi were designing courses at Southern Pines, North Carolina, and their influence was felt at the trials for the Pan American Games and elsewhere. De Némethy's course at Oak Brook, Illinois, was especially noteworthy and called attention to his ability. De Némethy was not yet affiliated with the USET in an official capacity, but his name was becoming known.

Most of the American jumpers at the Pan American Games were green and were eliminated. Mexico, Argentina, and Chile placed first, second, and third in jumping, beating out their North American competition.

SHOW JUMPING AND THE USET

THE NEW COACH

Something had to be done before the 1956 Olympics at Stockholm, and it was obvious that further training would be essential to the future success of the USET jumping team. It was at this point that Bertalan de Némethy came upon the scene in the role of coach. De Némethy's equestrian background gave him the training and discipline that had always been such a vital part of the cavalry and its riders. In addition, he had the ability to project this military influence to civilians, and more importantly, to individuals. In taking an approach that was midway between military discipline and American

De Némethy with the USET jumping team, Ostend, 1955. *Left to right*, McCashin, Steinkraus, Russell, and Wiley. *Courtesy of the USET/photograph by Jean Bridel*

individuality, de Némethy formed the basis of what was to eventually become known as the "Gladstone style"—an American way of riding. Since teams are never permanent, but selected periodically, de Némethy's personal touch and ability to deal with all kinds of mentalities and personalities were indeed an asset.

The new coach's first challenge was overwhelming. He had just five weeks in which to prepare twenty-five riders for the Tryon, North Carolina trials and to prove to General Guy V. Henry and his committee that they could be ready for the Olympics.

"I ignored the inexperience of the riders and concentrated on the horses, to make them like machines," de Némethy says. First he controlled their speed by means of rails—cavalletti—placed on the ground. Then he added fences, gradually working up to gymnastic stadium-type jumps, using gates, brush, stone walls, and oxers in place of the conventional rails. "I developed a kind of shortcut to get them 'through the mill.' It worked with at least half the riders," says de Némethy of his ingenious system, a system which arose from need and illustrated the old proverb that necessity is the mother of invention.

The Americans placed fifth out of twenty teams—out of the medals—but great improvement could be seen, and the stage was set for the future.

On the home front, when the Team first began to be invited to compete at the big national shows, it was not, at first, taken very seriously, especially by seasoned professionals. "But after we started to win, their attitude changed!" says de Némethy, smiling. "They didn't like to see 'little girls' like Mary Mairs and Kathy Kusner beating someone who had been making his living with horses for the past fifteen or twenty years."

As the Team continued to win, eyes were opened, and top trainers began to learn and observe. The difference between the old ways and the Team approach was that of trial and error versus systematic training. While there are still a few "natural" riders who are capable of learning solely by experience, most will benefit far more from classical, methodical

Kathy Kusner and Untouchable taking the Hickstead Bank, England, 1968. On the homefront, eyes were opened as Team members began to beat seasoned professionals. *Courtesy of the USET*

training, explains de Némethy. "There are always a few exceptions," he concedes, citing England's Harvey Smith as an example. "However," he adds, "even after so much success, he, too, realized that the horse would be better if someone made him more flexible, taught him all the elementary, proper signals. The logical, good methods can improve even the genius." De Némethy recalls seeing the British dressage coach riding Smith's horses for him in the mornings at Mexico City before the Olympics.

Under de Némethy's guidance, the old trial-and-error ways were gradually abandoned, and the training of jumpers began to reflect respect for the basics. While "dressage" was once a "dirty" word, associated with the circus, it has now become, thanks to de Némethy, a term that is interchanged with "elementary training" or "schooling on the flat," and the value of suppling exercises has been demonstrated by his methods.

As the Team improved and showed what it could do, it became a role model for all who aspired to success in the show ring. "Making the Team" has become the loftiest goal of even the youngest junior competitor.

The progress of horsemanship in the United States during the past twenty-five or thirty years has been called, by knowledgeable horsemen, nothing less than revolutionary. Our three-day teams have been victorious, and while we still have a long way to go in dressage, we are learning in much the same way as did our show jumping team. Team activities have spread their influence to all corners of the American equestrian community.

Had it not been for a group of farsighted, enthusiastic promoters of equestrian sports, international competition on the part of the United States might have ground to a halt with the disbanding of the U.S. Cavalry. Instead, the traditions that were upheld by the military have been continued. Furthermore, the importance of exposure to competition abroad—and not only in Olympic years—was emphasized by de Némethy early in his association with the USET. He helped to establish a precedent that would contribute to the growth of American equestrian knowledge in many areas.

Jack Fritz credits the USET as a prime force in the progress that has been made in all phases of our country's equestrian activities. It is in show jumping, however, that the changes have been most evident.

CHANGES

In recent years the sport has undergone changes, as indicated in Chapter 1, and so has the USET. The large prizes resulting from corporate sponsorships have kept horses jumping bigger fences and competing more frequently than ever before. In the

SHOW JUMPING AND THE USET

Frank Chapot and Anakonda at Hickstead, 1967. Exposure to international courses had a direct effect on American competition. *Courtesy of the USET/photograph by Jean Bridel*

United States, the sequence begins with the autumn horse shows (the Washington International, the National Horse Show in New York, and Toronto) and goes on to the Florida winter circuit (Palm Beach, Ocala, and Tampa) and the World Cup before competition in Europe. The horses grow tired by the end of the season.

Another problem is that we no longer have the control over the horses that we did in the past, but are subject to the wishes of the owners. In the early days of the USET, horses were loaned or donated to the Team, the riders were selected and assigned to their horses, and the situation was controlled. Selected riders spent several months or weeks training at Gladstone and always prepared the horses as final training before leaving for Europe or other international shows in the United States, such as Harrisburg, the Washington International, the National Horse Show, and Toronto. One or two of the younger riders who were selected were added to the older ones to join the squad for Europe or for other international competition as preparation for the Pan American Games and Olympics. Now, says de Némethy, they arrive just in time to leave for the competition. There is no simple solution, although de Némethy advises that we take a look at the French and German systems and try to adopt something similar. The French and German federations buy a partnership—a share in a horse that someone wants to sell—so that they have control over where the horse goes and what he does. As today's high standards make it increasingly difficult to keep horses sound and consistent, we have to continue to look for answers.

Too much competition is bad for young people, in de Némethy's opinion, and "will not improve their riding philosophy and approach." He points out that Germany, between the two world wars, was unbeatable; having lost many of their great course designers and teachers, they now rely more on the horses' natural abilities. Our American system of using hunter and equitation competition as preparation promotes good horses and riders, and its values should not be overlooked.

SHOW JUMPING AND THE USET

AN INSPIRATION

While many horses and riders have come and gone in de Némethy's years with the USET, he takes great pride in the fact that the Team's image has remained inspirational. In the early years of European competition, the other nations admired America's big, beautiful Thoroughbreds, their abilities, their easy and elegant performances, their riders' classic styles and relaxed confidence, and they were amazed at the patriotism, dedication, and discipline of the American competitors. They were always physically and mentally prepared, their equipment was immaculate, and riders and grooms alike took pride in what they did. In a film called *Equestrian Ambassadors*, made more than a decade ago, the American riders demonstrated themselves to be fine representatives of their country and were called by many "the best thing for the United States." Personal conflicts, drug abuse, alcohol, and other contemporary problems were conspicuously absent from the Team.

The Europeans wondered how de Némethy could be surrounded by such disciplined people. Early in his association, he had discovered the answer. He realized that the old-time attitude was inappropriate, since riders today do not have the same strong background as that of the military officers of his youth. All were equal in their desire to be the best and had to be treated accordingly. "You cannot overestimate or underestimate people too many times," says de Némethy, who tried to keep his judgment consistent. His role models were the cavalry officers that he had most admired in his academy days, and he strove to instill in his riders the same desire to please.

Although his own role with the USET has changed, de Némethy is hopeful that the traditions of the USET will continue. America has come a long way, and in that journey, the name of Bertalan de Némethy has become synonymous with show jumping and the USET.

4

At Home and Abroad

If you were to ask Bert de Némethy to name his most memorable experience in his years with the USET jumping team, he would probably reply, "The Munich Olympics." Never before were triumph and tragedy combined in so dramatic a way—triumph because to win the silver medal in a big equestrian country like Germany was in itself an accomplishment; tragedy because the gold was only ¼ fault away.

But the Olympics represent only one facet of the many kinds of competition faced by the Team. There were Nations Cup courses that were long and imposed tight time limits and problems to test the competitors' skill and judgment. Team competition at the Olympics has been held similarly to Nations Cup competition as of 1972 in Munich, with four riders participating and the best three scores in each round counting toward the total. American riders have been prominent at the Pan American Games and in the World Championships and have competed in Grand Prix jumping for large prizes at the best shows in the world. They have won the King George V Cup and the Queen Elizabeth II Cup, held at London's Royal International Horse Show and considered to be two of the most prestigious competitions for male and female riders, respectively. In CSIs such as the National Horse Show and Washington International, our Team has been outstanding (a CSI is a Concours Saute International or competition open to foreign riders who have been invited by the host country and authorized by their own federation to compete, organized with the permission of the Fédération Equestre Internationale and the corresponding national federation; a CSIO is a Concours Saute International Officiel or official international show at which a Nations Cup competition is held. Each country can hold only one per year except for the United States and Canada, which are permitted two because of their size).

In short, there have been so many competitions and such a long list of horses and riders during the de Némethy years, that it is difficult to include all without any oversights. From the early days to the present, the Team has distinguished itself both in the show ring and by its exemplary behavior.

Competition abroad is more feasible today because of the reduced travel time and discomfort with the advent of the modern jet airplane. Flying horses is still a risky business, but compared to years ago, there has been a vast improvement. Occasionally there will be a horse who does not appreciate air travel. Patrick Butler's Sloopy, ridden by Neal Shapiro, had to be sent back from the airport in 1970 because he began breaking out of his box. The following year he was shipped to Europe by boat from Newark, while the other horses were flown ahead. He first had to be familiarized with his box; then it was carefully prepared against destruction. "The dock workers must have thought a tiger was coming on board!" jokes de Némethy. Neal Shapiro and groom Peter Zeiler both became violently seasick, but Sloopy thrived. It was only later that de Némethy learned, much to his horror, that nobody had looked in on the horse for two or three days during the voyage. Fortunately, however, what seemed like a trip on the *Titanic* to his rider and groom was no major problem for Sloopy, who eventually went on to become a seasoned traveler.

AT HOME AND ABROAD

Sloopy, ridden by Neal Shapiro at Fontainebleau, 1971, became a seasoned traveler after a rocky beginning. *Courtesy of the USET*

EARLY COMPETITION

In de Némethy's early years as coach, his team members included William Steinkraus, Hugh Wiley, Frank Chapot, and George Morris, who were later joined by Mary Mairs and Kathy Kusner. De Némethy describes them as "cool and competent" under pressure and fondly remembers the great horses of those years: Master William, Sinjon, San Lucas, Nautical, Ksar d'Esprit, Tomboy, Snowbound, and Night Owl, among others.

Nautical, in fact, has a special story. In 1959 Walt Disney was filming *The Horse With the Flying Tail*, and camera crews followed the Team to Europe. Nautical held some glamor as

THE DE NÉMETHY YEARS

an equine subject, partly because he was a Palomino—unusual in European competition at that time—and partly because he had a habit of flipping his tail as he sailed over a fence, inspiring applause and laughter from the audience, until it became his trademark. Nobody knew why he did it, and as de Némethy says, "It's too bad he couldn't tell us."

Nautical had started his Team career as a rather difficult horse, apparently associating jumping with something unpleasant from his past. He had changed hands many times during his life before Wiley acquired him. De Némethy remembers him as "excitable, but not crazy; clever and strong." Says de Némethy, "He was the sweetest guy in the stable or in the plane or van, but when he saw a fence, he became excited." He was never dangerous, adds de Némethy, just highstrung. Patient schooling helped, and Nautical's jumping ability made him a valuable asset to the Team.

Hugh Wiley's Nautical achieved fame in Walt Disney's *Horse With the Flying Tail. Courtesy of the USET*

AT HOME AND ABROAD

The filming of the Disney movie presented problems. The filmmakers, says de Némethy, were "not the most relaxing people to have around." At Aachen, the unions did not want foreign filmmakers, and de Némethy found himself acting as translator and trying to keep everyone calm. While trying to concentrate on his horses and riders, de Némethy would be distracted by people giving him stage directions! The cameras followed Nautical in Europe, seeking victory, until the horse qualified for the George V Cup at the 1959 Royal International in London.

The drama was worthy of Disney. The competition was to be televised; the royal box was full; the course appeared difficult. Nautical jumped the first round with no faults, and the tension grew as he entered the arena the second time. Spain's Paco Goyoaga had had a clear round, which was matched by Nautical, precipitating a jump-off against the clock. This time Goyoaga's horse incurred 8 jumping faults. In a brilliant finish, Nautical won the class and the trophy, captured on film for posterity.

The movie was a big success, and de Némethy agrees that it gave the Team good publicity. Nautical died in retirement on Hugh Wiley's Virginia farm, but today a large oil painting of him stands in the USET office at Gladstone, a reminder of his talent and beauty.

Despite the pressures of competing during the making of the movie, Wiley remembers that show and the winning of the George V Cup as one of the highlights of his riding career. Another memorable occasion was winning the Nations Cup in Rome in 1959 with Steinkraus, Chapot, and Morris. It was one year before the Olympics, a year in which they were training and competing in Europe over difficult courses and in strong competition, and it was also their first time in Rome. The setting, too, was memorable: the beautiful Piazza de Siena in the Villa Borghese.

THE DE NÉMETHY YEARS

An American victory in the Rome Prize of Nations in 1959 was a great satisfaction to coach de Némethy and his riders. *Courtesy of the USET*

THE RIDERS

Steinkraus, Wiley, and Chapot were longtime Team members at a time when there was not the frequent turnover there is today. Wiley rode with the Team for eight years. The year-after-year training produced a strong team of people who rode in the same style—Wiley likes to call it the "de Némethy style"—and their coach's unselfish dedication was unmatched anywhere else in the world. Wiley credits the repetitious, systematic training with the riders' success, recalling that they were lunged for fifteen to thirty minutes every day in a dressage seat to achieve deep, secure seats. Today, he reflects, the methods are the same, but the horses and riders keep changing. Wiley's Team experience remained with him long after he ceased to compete; he found de Némethy's words coming back to him in much the same way that they guided him through his training. Says Wiley, "As you're riding, you 'feel' his words."

Wiley had ridden all his life, but claims, "I learned most of what I know from de Némethy. I had some natural talent, and I was competing and winning, but I didn't know a thing about the *art* of riding until I got on the Team." In 1958 he won the King George V Cup on Master William, retaining it with his 1959 victory on Nautical, and in 1960 he was seventh individually at the Rome Olympics on Master William. Nautical, his versatile Palomino, won in speed classes, Puissance, and even in a High Jump Over Poles, forerunner of the Puissance, in its last time held in Ballsbridge, Ireland, in 1958. In 1959 he jumped two clear rounds in the Nations Cup at Rome toward the American victory and cleaned up at London's Royal International, winning the King George V, *Horse and Hound*, and *Daily Mail* cups. Ksar d'Esprit, who was ridden by William Steinkraus, had been bred on Wiley's family farm. Having had the opportunity to view show jumping on a grand, international scale, Wiley concludes that de Némethy's methods combine classical principles with the best European traditions.

William Steinkraus's association with de Némethy is one of many years' standing. Steinkraus is a former president of the USET, and his own contributions have been numerous. He and Arthur McCashin were successful open jumper riders who represented the United States at Helsinki in 1952. Steinkraus first met Bertalan de Némethy more than thirty years ago and watched him compete (and win) at Devon in 1953. As he became better acquainted with him, he recognized de Némethy's abilities and knew that they would benefit the USET. In fact, says Steinkraus, de Némethy's high standards were quite compatible with McCashin's; both were fastidious in stable care and management and both were excellent horsemen in all respects.

Steinkraus had already started to work in a direction similar to the de Némethy approach, though independently.

His idealism and values were similar, perhaps because good horsemen share a certain common perfectionistic goal. "I was his kind of rider even before I met him," explains Steinkraus, adding that de Némethy was an important person in his evolution as a rider. He also gained a valuable and enduring friendship. Both are involved with and dedicated to the USET today, although in different roles from the ones they occupied as rider and coach.

Frank Chapot spent many years as a member of the USET jumping team and in 1965 married fellow team member Mary Mairs. Among his many successes were the silver team medal in Rome in 1960 riding Trail Guide; numerous international class and Nations Cup wins on Mrs. John Galvin's San Lucas, as well as placing fourth individually at the 1968 Olympics, only seconds away from a medal; and

William Steinkraus on Mainspring at Lucerne, 1972. Steinkraus and de Némethy established an enduring friendship. *Courtesy of the USET*

memorable performances with such horses as Cheeca Farm's Good Twist, Mainspring (donated to the USET by William D. Haggard III), Anakonda, White Lightning, Manon, and Viscount.

"The thing that Bert always had was a lot of class," Chapot emphasizes. "He was always a gentleman and could deal with horse owners and team members, even if they were difficult and demanding. He never lost his cool." He hopes that some of this attitude has rubbed off on him in his life today as a rider, teacher, trainer, and course designer. "Very few people teach the lessons Bert has taught," he adds, describing the immaculate turnout of Team horses and riders. "It is very important to know how to represent your country. I hope this will carry over for years to come."

Chapot has maintained a close friendship with de Némethy over the years, which his wife believes is stronger now than ever. Team loyalty and respect for the man who played so important a role have not diminished, but echo the feeling of those earlier years.

CONTINUED IMPROVEMENT

Under de Némethy's guidance, the Team continued to improve and to win during the late 1950's. In October 1959, the Americans won the gold medal at the Pan American Games. Though diehards pointed out that there was no European competition at the Pan Am Games, the Team had already achieved success in Europe earlier in the year, winning thirteen team classes. Frank Chapot won the Championship of Brussels, George Morris the Grand Prix at Ostend, Steinkraus the German championship, and Wiley had had six wins.

In 1959 the USET Jumping Team won on the fall circuit at Washington, New York, and Toronto. At New York's National Horse Show, the Americans took the Team Championship, and captain William Steinkraus won the individual championship and the newly inaugurated German Challenge Trophy. Riviera Wonder, ridden by Steinkraus, made a suc-

Frank Chapot on San Lucas at Lucerne, 1972. Chapot was a member of the Pan American Games Gold Medal Team of 1963. *Courtesy of the USET*

cessful comeback after suffering a recurring injury; he won the Royce A. Drake Memorial Challenge Trophy and the Individual Championship Challenge Trophy and made headlines in the New York papers.

The 1960 annual meeting of the USET was held January 7 to 9 in Detroit in conjunction with the AHSA convention. Fund raising and plans for the 1960 Olympics at Rome were among the topics of discussion. The Team spent most of the winter schooling at the Boulder Brook Club in Scarsdale, New

York. Tryouts were held there while the "old campaigners" rested at Tryon, North Carolina, including Diamant, Ksar d'Esprit, First Boy, Master William, Nautical, Night Owl, Riviera Wonder, and Trail Guide. At Boulder Brook were Steinkraus's Wonabet, Miss E. R. Sears' Southern Squirrel, Trish Galvin's Tally Ho, Mrs. Ernest Mahler's Silverminer, Mrs. Walter B. Devereaux's Sinbad, Mrs. A. C. Randolph's Palomino High Noon, Cappy Smith's Reflector, S. R. Currier's Cin-a-Bit, and two new horses owned by Arthur McCashin, Gold Lodge and Silver City. Steinkraus and de Némethy worked together with the horses and were assisted by George Morris and Hugh Wiley, who came as often as time allowed, and Frank Chapot, who joined them on weekends.

While most of the international jumpers of recent years have been Thoroughbreds, in the early years of competition they attracted special attention. Cross-breds or coldbloods were most commonly seen. Marie C. Lafrenz noted in the *New York Herald Tribune* of March 6, 1960 the increase in the number of Thoroughbred Team horses. Andante, Riviera Wonder, and Toytown were registered Thoroughbreds, while others, such as Windsor Castle and Nautical, had Thoroughbred sires. Thoroughbreds, it was pointed out, had the speed, heart, and flexibility so necessary to an international jumper. In 1959 seven out of eight USET jumpers were Thoroughbreds, and the eighth, Nautical, was sired by a Thoroughbred. In 1952 at Helsinki, the Americans were riding German warmbloods that they had acquired from the army, although William Steinkraus's mount was an off-track Thoroughbred.

Another point of interest raised by Mrs. Lafrenz was the amateur-versus-professional question. In the *New York Herald Tribune* of April 10, 1960, she drew comparisons between William Steinkraus and professional horseman Harry de Leyer of Long Island. Steinkraus's main goal was to win for the United States, and in so doing, he faced tough foreign competition over difficult courses. De Leyer, who was earning his living from horses, had a much heavier schedule, which included hunting and instructing in addition to showing (he was winning in those years on Snow Man and other horses). The conclusion reached was that each man was the best for the job he was doing, and that, while de Leyer might find Steinkraus's shows quite a strain, Steinkraus would likewise find de Leyer's tight schedule exhausting.

There were some professionals who resented the fact that European methods were being used on American horses. Because of the difference in show conditions at home and abroad, systematic, long-range training was necessary for success, as opposed to the "get-quick-results" philosophy of domestic competition. The old ways were impractical, and as the Team continued to compete in Europe, it became more and more evident that de Némethy's system was the best.

THE SIXTIES

The 1960 Team in Europe consisted of William Steinkraus, Hugh Wiley, Frank Chapot, and George Morris. George Morris had joined the Team following a good basic background of show jumping and equitation and study with Gordon Wright, Otto Heuckeroth, and other leading professionals. De Némethy exposed him to a sophisticated world of riding that included cavalletti work and, as Morris says, "opened up a whole new world regarding the refinements of riding." These refinements topped off the practical experience that he had gained in his years of showing and hunting, and he later went on to study with Gunnar Anderson and other dressage people abroad—an education made possible, he explains, "because of Bert."

In his four years with the USET, George Morris had many successes: leading rider at Lucerne, winner of the *Horse and Hounds* Cup at White City, fourth individually at the Rome Olympics, and winner of many Grand Prix jumping events. Although today he considers himself "more of a teacher than a winner," his career was impressive. To him, the highlights were winning at Aachen in 1960 and at Dublin in 1958.

AT HOME AND ABROAD

At Lucerne he was the best placed rider in the show and won the Coup Vetivier.

The 1960 European calendar was a full one for Steinkraus, Wiley, Chapot, Morris, and their twelve horses. They schooled and conditioned at Munich in May, competed at Wiesbaden, Germany, and Lucerne in June, went on to White City (London), Aachen, Ostend, and Munich in July prior to the Rome Olympics, and following the Olympics, competed at the World Championships in Venice in September before returning home for the fall circuit.

De Némethy was quoted as saying that he felt the Team might take third in the Olympics (they were second). Their strongest opponents were the Germans and Italians. Aachen represented a great success for the Americans, who took the top three placings in the Grand Prix: Morris on Night Owl was first, Steinkraus on Ksar d'Esprit second, and Chapot on Tally Ho third. Steinkraus won the Puissance with Ksar d'Esprit and tied for first with Morris in another event. George Morris won a time class with High Noon and took two blues with Sinjon.

At the White City Show, Queen Elizabeth II presented the *Horse and Hounds* Cup to George Morris and Sinjon, and the Team won the Prince of Wales Cup.

The World Championships brought about a stroke of bad luck. Steinkraus, who was in the lead, drew David Broome's Sansalve as his last horse. It was a difficult mount, but they had a clear round. After the last fence, the horse slipped and fell upon landing, and Steinkraus suffered a broken collar bone, which put him out of commission for the fall shows. In spite of this mishap, the European tour was viewed as an overall triumph. Looking back, says George Morris, he realizes how "lucky" he was; yet the success of the American Team had more to do with skill and training than with luck.

Morris, Wiley, and Chapot went on to compete on the fall circuit of 1960, which was marked by tragedy when Trail Guide died in the midst of international competition at the National Horse Show. The USET, however, made a clean sweep of the shows at Harrisburg, Washington, New York, and Toronto, which, on top of their silver medal at the Olympics, made 1960 a year to remember.

The year 1961 found the USET in its new home at Gladstone. Young riders trained there, and trials were held in June and July, followed by an intensive course for sixteen selected riders in August. It was becoming evident that new blood was needed. Steinkraus had married in December 1960 and was pursuing a business career, Wiley and Chapot were also occupied with business careers, and George Morris was studying drama. Thirty-two riders were at Gladstone in June, and de Némethy presided over seven additional selection trials throughout the country. At Gladstone, he and three-day coach Stefan von Visy made written evaluations of each rider.

The year 1961 also saw a large increase in money prizes for show jumping. The Sands Point Horse Show offered a $1,000 jumper stake, and Ox Ridge and Fairfield each offered $5,000 in open jumping prize money. The National Horse Show was billed as "the world's richest International Jumping Stake," according to Marie Lafrenz in the *New York Herald Tribune*. The $7,500 stake sponsored by the United States Lines represented an increase of $6,500 over 1960 and more money than that offered at the Hamburg Derby and the Aachen International Stake. Show jumping was on its way to becoming big business!

The Seventy-eighth National Horse Show in November 1961 was a preview of things to come. Neal Shapiro, sixteen, won the PHA (Professional Horsemen's Association) class on Uncle Max on Saturday night, and Bernie Traurig, also sixteen, won both the Medal and Maclay finals that year. (Steinkraus had acknowledged Traurig as the junior with the most potential at the Thomas School of Horsemanship's Junior Olympics in April 1961.) Riviera Wonder won the Puissance over Windsor Castle, Snow Man, and McLain Street, clearing the wall at 6 feet 9 inches after five jump-offs.

New talent continued to appear in the early sixties. Mary Mairs joined the Team in 1962 at age eighteen, after winning the Pacific Coast Hunter Seat Championship in 1958 and the

Maclay finals in 1960. She became the first woman to win an individual gold medal at the Pan American Games at Sao Paulo, Brazil, in 1963, in addition to the team gold won with William Steinkraus and Frank Chapot. Tomboy, her chestnut mare, won the jumper stake and was Grand Champion at the Washington International in 1962, and the Team won the Nations Cups at New York, Harrisburg, and Toronto that fall.

Neal Shapiro was named to the Team in 1964 in a surprise switch at the National Horse Show. De Némethy announced Mary Mairs's withdrawal because Tomboy was lame, and Shapiro, with Uncle Tom and Jacks or Better, joined the squad that consisted of William Steinkraus with San Lucas and Snowbound, Frank Chapot with Manon and Shady Lake, and Kathy Kusner and Untouchable. Kathy Kusner was another noteworthy addition to the Team, coming from riding for horse dealers to the polished de Némethy approach and going on to chalk up many victories.

The 1964 fall circuit was eyed with reservations on the part of de Némethy. He reported that the horses and riders were tired from their long journey to and from the Tokyo Olympics, but told the newspapers, "I think we'll give a good account of ourselves." Canada was especially strong, having won the team championship at Harrisburg, and Mexico and Argentina were also competing at the National Horse Show. Tired or not, the Americans won the Nations Cup once again! Kathy Kusner won three blues and the individual championship, and the United States was 49 points ahead of Canada, in second place, with a total of 135 points. Steinkraus won the Puissance and tied for second individually with Canada's Tom Gayford, and Shapiro was second in the Puissance and Grand Prix de New York. The United States went on to win seven out of ten events and the team championship at Toronto's Royal Winter Fair.

The following year, the USET jumpers won thirty-three out of forty classes on the fall circuit. Mary Mairs had married Frank Chapot, and both were team members, along with Kathy Kusner and William Steinkraus. One of the more dramatic moments of the season occurred when Steinkraus and Kusner were tied for first place, individually. Trying to beat Kathy Kusner's fast time, Steinkraus almost took a spill when Snowbound stumbled, losing his hunt cap and becoming unseated. He somehow managed to get himself back in the saddle and finish in 38.6 seconds to win.

According to USET spokesmen, 1965 was the Team's best showing in its fifteen years of existence. This was both an evaluation and a look at what was to come. In 1965 the FEI initiated the President's Cup or International Team Jumping Championship. It was open to any country represented in Nations Cup competition by a minimum of six riders throughout the course of a year, based on a points system (in case of a tie, the number of first place wins would determine the victor). Although the United States team was not among the top six in that first year, it had the highest total points in 1966 and 1968 and was thereafter prominent in the placings, enjoying special success in Nations Cup competition on the North American fall circuit.

SUCCESS AND CHANGES

This success continued well into the 1970's, including numerous Nations Cup wins throughout the decade. In 1975 Michael Matz, Dennis Murphy, Joe Fargis, and Buddy Brown won the team gold at the Pan American Games at Mexico City, followed by yet another team gold at the Pan American Games in 1979, this time with Buddy Brown, Melanie Smith, Michael Matz, and Norman dello Joio taking the victory gallop. New horses and riders came along, but the team remained strong.

As Frank Chapot sees it, the turnover of riders in recent years stems from the fact that there are simply more "replacements" (good riders) available, with good horses and good coaching behind them. "We don't need a coach as we did when we were first starting," he explains. "Today, riders like Katie Monahan, Rodney Jenkins, Melanie Smith, Norman dello Joio, and others come to the Team well prepared. Our needs have changed."

AT HOME AND ABROAD

Carol Hofmann on San Pedro, Aachen, 1967. The USET was prominent in Nations Cup competition in the late 1960s. *Courtesy of the USET*

Looking back on the early days, Chapot remembers how greatly American competition differed from European. "Very few could make the Team," he says, "and when they did, they would stay longer. Now we have more depth; we are playing the same game as the Europeans."

Chrystine Jones, director of show jumping activities for the USET, points out that we still lack the big permanent outdoor stadiums of the Europeans, although we have excelled

Michael Matz riding Grande in Mexico. Matz was twice a member of the gold medal team at the Pan American Games. *Courtesy of the USET*

in indoor competition, winning the World Cup three times out of four. Jones rode with the Team from 1965 to 1967 and is today acknowledged as a leading course designer. "My exposure to Bert was timely," she says. She had been started by his good friend Gabor Foltenyi, and her experience with de Némethy was "the polishing of the apple." Her interest in course design grew as she walked and analyzed European courses with him, and she began to design courses herself in the late 1960's. "Bert certainly opened the door as far as my course designing career is concerned," she asserts. "It is still a learning experience to ride and walk courses with him." Like many other former Team riders, she has maintained a lasting friendship with de Némethy. "He is someone I've been very fortunate to know in my lifetime," she says.

Jones views the changes that occurred during the late 1960's and into the 1970's as a result of the development of the American Grand Prix show jumping circuit and the lessening need for a team coach as horse owners and sponsors provided what was formerly provided by the Team. People who considered their horses a potential investment and took pride in their achievements were not as likely to donate them to the Team as they once were. Horses and riders now come to the Team already well prepared.

By the time de Némethy was ready to "retire" from his role as coach, the Team was in a better position to relinquish him. He had established a good foundation, and as the Team's needs changed, de Némethy was able to serve in other ways both at home and abroad.

Not all of de Némethy's travels have been connected with the Team. He has officiated at shows and conducted clinics in riding and course design all over the world, often in interesting settings and sometimes under unusual circumstances. December 1958, for example, found him in Havana, Cuba, where he gave a clinic and attended the inauguration of the Club Hípico Costa Azúl de Alamar at the invitation of its president, Luis de La Valette, who had met de Némethy while captaining the Cuban team at the National Horse Show that

November. While Cuba struggled with internal political turmoil, de Némethy was enjoying the sunshine and parties, combining business with pleasure. Just before New Year, he was warned by de La Valette of rumors that Castro planned to march into Havana on January 1, 1959. If he did not leave immediately, he risked being detained. "I missed my New Year's Eve party," de Némethy laments, but he left on December 31 without encountering any difficulty and was far from Havana by the time the Castro takeover occurred.

As a world traveler, Bertalan de Némethy has been a fine representative for show jumping, as well as an unofficial American ambassador. Uninvolved with politics and petty gossip, he has always inspired admiration and has set an example for those around him. In his own subtle way, he has established a code of conduct that lends dignity to the sporting world and affects its participants on an international scale.

5

The Olympics and the Pan American Games

The Olympic Games have always symbolized the ultimate in athletic achievements and goals. To earn a berth on an Olympic team is the fondest dream of every starry-eyed, sports-minded youngster, and our Olympians enjoy a kind of hero worship not unlike that of matinee idols and rock stars. The rivalry between nations often parallels world politics. Fans take pride in the number of medals accumulated, celebrate the Bruce Jenners and the Mark Spitzes, and thrill to the playing of the national anthem following a victory.

Equestrian sports differ from others, since horse and rider form a team and must perform in unison, animal and human attuned to one another. As the result of years of practice, their means of communication is almost invisible to the onlooker. Each of the disciplines—show jumping, dressage and three-day—reflects skill, dedication, and a merging of talents that is, unfortunately, too often overlooked by the television camera. A few minutes in the Olympic spotlight can culminate either in glory or disappointment. Equestrians often participate in more than one Olympic competition, unlike many other athletes, since the age factor is not as important as in other sports. John Winnett made the transition from World Championship show jumping to Olympic dressage, and William Steinkraus is a veteran of no less than six Olympic squads.

THE DE NÉMETHY YEARS

Bertalan de Némethy seemed destined for the Olympics, when, as a member of the Hungarian show jumping team, he was considered a good prospect for the 1940 Olympic Games. Between 1937 and 1940 he competed at many CHIOs in Aachen, Lucerne, Munich, Rome, Florence, and Vienna with fellow teammates Valko, Plattny, and d'Endrody. World War II ended their Olympic hopes, when the Games were canceled.

Many years later, de Némethy made it to the Olympics—not as a contender, but as mentor to a newly organized American squad. Today it is almost a full-time commitment to become a champion, but in those days, all of the riders were amateurs who were involved in other things in addition to the sport. Many had to quit their jobs or leave their homes and farms to go to Europe for early preparation for the 1956 Olympics. Steinkraus was the only member of the Team with previous Olympic experience, having ridden with McCashin and Russell to win a team bronze in 1952 at Helsinki.

STOCKHOLM

Stockholm was a memorable first Olympic experience for de Némethy. In Stockholm, he remembers, the equestrians were the "big guys." Other sports, such as swimming and track and field, took place in Melbourne, Australia. Equestrians had the limelight and the full attention of the press in Stockholm. Furthermore, King Gustav of Sweden was deeply interested in horses, so the competition had a special style and glamor, as well as an excellent, well-designed course, which de Némethy recalls was demanding and a bit severe for the Prize of Nations. The stadium was small, accommodating only 45,000 to 50,000 spectators.

All scores counted individually at Stockholm, although only team medals were presented. The Americans had only been practicing under de Némethy's coaching for a year, and as de Némethy puts it, "We were a little too inexperienced." Hugh Wiley was riding Trail Guide, because Nautical was

THE OLYMPICS AND THE PAN AMERICAN GAMES

Riding at Stockholm, 1956; *left to right*, Frank Chapot, Hugh Wiley, William Steinkraus, and Bertalan de Némethy. *Courtesy of Bertalan de Némethy*

recovering from a hoof injury. William Steinkraus rode Night Owl and Frank Chapot competed on Belair.

The Americans made a good showing, placing fifth out of seventeen nations. The gold medal went to West Germany, the silver to Italy, and the bronze to Great Britain. Individual medals were not awarded. In the individual standings, however, Hugh Wiley was number eleven.

ROME

By the time the 1960 Olympics at Rome rolled around, the American team had become far stronger and more experienced. Individual placings were counted, in addition to team standings, for the first time.

The setting was artistic, and de Némethy remembers being surrounded by people and color. "It doesn't matter what you are doing in Rome," he declares. "It is such a fascinating place, and the Italians have such terrific taste! It was very glamorous and beautiful—one of the loveliest places in the world."

A change of horses in midstream, so to speak, found William Steinkraus riding Ksar d'Esprit and Hugh Wiley on Master William, considered by de Némethy to be one of the best horses he ever trained. Frank Chapot and George Morris were the other two members of the squad.

In spite of Raimondo d'Inzeo's individual medal and great performance, the Americans took the silver team medal behind Germany and ahead of the Italian team's bronze. George Morris was only one point away from the individual bronze medal, and Hugh Wiley was seventh. Rome was indeed a feather in American caps.

TOKYO

"Tokyo was most interesting for everyone," says de Némethy of the setting for the 1964 Olympic Games. The fascinating difference in culture and people, however, was offset by the difficulties in getting around in Tokyo, in communicating, and in understanding the Oriental mentality.

De Némethy feels that the Japanese organized the Games for political reasons, to prove that they belonged among the civilized societies of the world, to forget the war, and to show the West that they could do things not only as well, but better. They went all out to make an impression, providing well-dressed, multilingual ticket takers at the stadium and trying to anticipate the every need of their guests.

Horses were vanned to three or four designated schooling areas every day. Each team had to sign up in the evening to select the location of its choice, indicating the desired time and how many horses they were bringing. "This led to misunderstanding and intrigue," relates de Némethy. At dinner, the

Bertalan de Némethy exercising a horse at Stockholm, 1956. Stockholm was his first venture as coach of the USET. *Courtesy of Bertalan de Némethy*

chefs d'equipe would try to second-guess each other, and the Japanese would try to be a step ahead so as not to lose face. On one occasion, for example, the U.S. team had decided to cancel out on a schooling site because of expected rain. Next morning, however, the van was ready and waiting—"just in case you changed your mind."

Steady rain made the course treacherous and caused the horses to sink six inches into the ground. Mary Mairs and Tomboy had an unaccustomed refusal because the horse was afraid to take off under the slippery conditions. It was the kind of situation that cannot be anticipated until it occurs. This, explains de Némethy, is where "mileage," or experience in all kinds of footing, under all kinds of conditions, pays off. The average outsider or horse owner isn't aware of the importance of this experience until a situation arises such as the one faced by Mary Mairs and Tomboy; then it is not enough simply to be in good form. Tokyo is a good example of the unexpected that may occur and cause disappointment in the world of show jumping. The American team was strong, and Mary Mairs and Tomboy were consistent and successful competitors, yet they had six fences down in the first round.

"The mare was as well prepared as she could have been," Mary Mairs Chapot remembers today, pointing out that the poor footing, coupled with other factors, simply caused her to "give up."

West Germany, France, and Italy placed first, second, and third, and no medals were taken home by the Americans. While the trip was long and tiring and the results disappointing, the experience was nonetheless of value, if only to serve as a reminder to anticipate the unexpected in international competition.

MEXICO

In terms of the unexpected, no other Olympic competition could have been as frustrating as the one held in Mexico in

1968. De Némethy remembers the course as "almost impossible to ride" and considers the event a "disaster," in spite of William Steinkraus's individual gold medal.

Preparations for Mexico began at least a year in advance. Professional people and veterinarians from all over the world studied the climate and altitude to determine the effects they might have on horses and humans. Horses were sent to Mexico

Triple Crown, led by George Simmons, arrives in Mexico in 1968 as de Némethy looks on. *Courtesy of the USET*

twenty-eight days before the competition, kept in top condition, hand walked daily for one week, and then gradually exercised until five days before. This is contrary to the procedure for race horses, points out de Némethy, who are flown down, raced, and taken right home again with no time allowed for acclimation. In anticipation of the Olympics, however, some countries actually sent their horses ahead a year in advance to ensure their readiness.

Canada, the winning team, accumulated an unprecedented 110 faults. The United States placed fourth behind Canada, France, and West Germany. According to William Steinkraus, "The character of the event was destroyed by the technical circumstances." The fences were big and came down too easily, the time limit was too tight, and distances were awkward. Steinkraus points out that by using all of the ingredients of course design at the same time and combining difficulties of line, time, and other factors, the course designer wound up building something that nobody could jump. Consequently, the competition at Mexico did not resemble the sport with which the riders were acquainted, but became more or less a matter of survival. Competitors had an average of eight fences down, or 30 faults, which left a bad taste.

The individual course, fortunately, was better, or, as Steinkraus expresses it, "within the frame of the previous Olympic results in terms of the number and distribution of faults." Steinkraus took the individual gold medal over Britain's Marion Coakes, silver, and David Broome, bronze, which made the whole experience more palatable for the Americans. Steinkraus, however, says that both he and de Némethy always cherished team medals over individual and admits that his greatest ambition would have been to captain the gold medal team. Nevertheless, his Olympic gold was a first for the American jumping team and a source of pride to its fans.

MUNICH

The United States came closest to an Olympic gold team medal in Munich in 1972. "We almost had it in our hands," sighs de Némethy. It was sad to lose by only ¼ of a time fault; at the same time, it was thrilling to be so close to Germany, the home country and one of the strongest equestrian nations, in front of 80,000 spectators.

If Steinkraus, the last rider, had gone clean, the Americans would have had the gold. "You could hear the crowd holding its breath," describes de Némethy. "When his horse put a foot in the water, there was a huge collective gasp." Steinkraus has never felt bad about it, however, for he honestly did not think he had a chance of jumping two clean rounds and was in fact pleased with Mainspring's performance. To say years later, "If only Neal Shapiro had been a second quicker, for a tie, or two seconds quicker to win" or "If only Steinkraus had had a clear round" is somewhat contrary to the nature of the sport, in which there is always an element of suspense.

In spite of the dual view of Munich as both success and disappointment, it should be pointed out that the Germans had the advantage of being more involved with show jumping as a national sport. German riders frequently appear on the covers of national magazines, whereas, in the United States, says Steinkraus, such a thing is unheard of—unless, perhaps, you are murdered by a terrorist! "Hans Winkler was more than a sports figure," he says. "He was a national figure." Successful American riders, unfortunately, do not enjoy the recognition accorded other outstanding athletes. Even within certain equestrian circles, the names of prominent jumper riders may draw blank stares.

Steinkraus feels that the United States has been more successful in bringing its best to the Olympic Games than some other strong equestrian nations, such as Germany, who make their trials tougher than the Games themselves. This, he says, is an argument in favor of a selection committee, which can use its discretion and intelligence as opposed to a computer or adding machine in deciding who goes to the Olympics. In general, he observes, nations make a big effort for the Olympics because of the prestige gained by an Olympic victory. "A real Olympic course," he says, "is the hardest one they build in the forty-eight months between Games." He compares it to asking a 100-meter dash man to run 150 meters, adding, "Equestrian competitors, not knowing in advance what the course is going to be, come to the Games wondering

Neal Shapiro and Sloopy, Munich, 1972. In addition to a Team silver, this pair took an individual bronze medal at the Munich Olympics. *Courtesy of the USET*

what game they are going to play, not knowing the degree of difficulty or the real content. That is almost unique, facing the unknown in that way. The three-day and jumper people have to be ready for anything—that is, anything within the rules."

Neal Shapiro and Sloopy won the bronze medal at Munich, giving additional prestige to the team silver won with fellow team members William Steinkraus, Kathy Kusner, and Frank Chapot. Kathy Kusner was tenth individually on Fleet Apple. Fifty-four individual competitors from twenty-one countries participated, fifteen of which had the full complement of three riders, making Munich one of the biggest Olympic jumping competitions ever. The individual gold went to Italy's Graziano Mancinelli on Ambassador and the silver to Ann Moore of Great Britain on Psalm.

MONTREAL

The results of the Montreal Olympics of 1976 were somewhat similar to those of the 1982 World Championships, with the Americans placing fourth. Frank Chapot, who was the only American rider with previous Olympic experience, placed fifth individually. Heavy rains on new turf made for difficult footing, or as Chapot calls it, a "flukey situation." The remaining members of the team—Buddy Brown, Robert Ridland, and Michael Matz—were newcomers to Olympic competition. Because of the rain-soaked ground and insufficient drainage, the Bromont course had to be revised to what some coaches called a "Mickey Mouse" course; yet there were still no clear rounds in the Prize of Nations. While the American team fared better in the second round than in the first, it could not recover enough to catch France, Germany, and Canada. As viewed by Frank Chapot, since the Team had been doing well in other Nations Cup competitions that year, being out of the medals at the Olympics was actually an exception to its general overall success. (Chapot himself had encountered special difficulties in the second round of the team competition, having lost his glasses—on which he is quite dependent—over the second element of the fourth fence. He nevertheless put in a good round with only 4 faults.)

Two silver team medals, one gold, and one bronze during the de Némethy years of Olympic competition certainly indicate hope for the future. Perhaps the dream shared by de Némethy and Steinkraus of a team victory will become a reality.

THE PAN AMERICAN GAMES

Like the Olympics, the Pan American Games are held every four years. Originally planned in the 1930's, they did not make their debut until 1951, following World War II, at which time they were deemed a big success, thanks to spectator interest and a touch of glamor provided by Argentinian hosts Juan and Eva Perón. The United States did not compete, since the USET had been formed only a year earlier. Chile was clearly the big winner in jumping, beating Argentina and Mexico, the latter having won at the 1948 Olympics. Chilean Alberto Larraguibel was the individual gold medalist; two years before, he had set a world record in high jumping of 8 feet 1¼ inches or 2.47 meters. Argentina's Carlos Delia took the silver medal, and Joaquin Larrain and Ricardo Echevarría tied for the bronze, though some records show Chile's Larrain as the official third place winner. The South American teams were strong at that time. Echevarría's horse Bambi went on to place second in the 1952 Olympics under Oscar Cristi. The Mexican team appeared without their famous rider Humberto Mariles, whose gold medal horse Arete, ridden by Alberto Valdes, placed fourteenth.

The year 1955 found the second Pan American Games in Mexico City. The only gold medal won by the USET was in three-day by Walter Staley on Mud Dauber. The American jumping team got off to a less-than-brilliant beginning, the selection trials having taken place in heavy rains. Team captain John R. Wheeler and William Steinkraus were both eliminated, and the other two team members, Charles Dennehy and Arthur McCashin, placed eighth and ninth respectively. Mexico won the team gold and the individual gold and bronze medals, prompting protests of favoritism on the part of the Mexican organizers. These complaints were never verified, and the Mexican team did not compete at the 1956 Olympics the next year to show what it could or could not do.

After this disappointing showing by the American jumping team, Bertalan de Némethy was engaged as coach. Within two and a half years, the team had achieved success and the recognition it was to enjoy for many years.

STRONG CONTENDER

The 1959 Pan American Games were hosted by the United States in Chicago. By now the American jumping squad and become one of the strongest contenders. William Steinkraus, Frank Chapot, Hugh Wiley, and George Morris won the team gold with 32 faults over Brazil, in second place with 59, and Chile, third with 80¾. For some unexplained reason, individual medals were not awarded. If they had been, America would have made a clean sweep, for Wiley, Chapot, and Steinkraus were first, second, and third. The United States had a gold medal in dressage to applaud, won by Patricia Galvin on Rath Patrick, while the American three-day team placed second to Canada. Galvin repeated her success four years later at Sao Paolo, Brazil.

At Sao Paolo in 1963, Steinkraus and Sinjon were leading after the first round of jumping with only 4 faults. Sinjon injured himself leaving the stadium and was unable to jump in the second round. Mary Mairs, riding Tomboy, became the first woman to win a Pan American gold jumping medal (she had been behind Steinkraus with 5¾ faults), while the silver medal went to Carlos Delia of Argentina and the bronze to Americo Simonetti of Chile. The American team won the team gold medal with 44¼ faults over Argentina, second with 52½ and Chile, third with 69. Six teams had competed; Mexico was fourth, Brazil fifth, and Uruguay was eliminated.

After its two-time winning streak, the American jumping team experienced disappointment at Winnipeg, Canada, in 1967, finishing second in the Nations Cup and winning no individual medals. Brazil was the surprise winner, with Canada third. Kathy Kusner, with 4 faults, qualified for the third place jump-off, but wound up in fifth place. Mary Mairs Chapot and Frank Chapot tied for seventh with 8 faults apiece, while William Steinkraus, with 12 faults, placed ninth individually. It was said that the loss of the gold medal was not due to an off day by a single rider, as in the Tokyo Olympics, but was the result of a series of knockdowns by all of the team members. On the brighter side, the American three-day team won the team gold, and American Kyra Downton rode Kadett to win the individual gold dressage medal.

The United States did not attend the 1971 Pan American Games at Cali, Colombia, because of warnings of the presence of Venezuelan equine encephamyelitis (VEE) infection, although Canadian veterinarians reported having seen no cases since 1968. Canada won all three team medals, the gold in dressage (Christilot Hanson), silver in three-day (Clint Banbury), and bronze in jumping (Torchy Millar on Le Dauphin).

The Americans bounced back to take gold team medals in all three disciplines at the 1975 Pan American Games in Mexico. Jumping teams from the United States, Brazil, Mexico, Canada, Venezuela, Guatemala, and San Salvador competed in the Pan American Prize of Nations. At the end of the first round, the United States had a total score (best three out of four) of 32 points and was narrowly holding the lead. Numerous knockdowns or faults were incurred by Michael Matz and Grande, Dennis Murphy and Dudley Do Right, and Joe Fargis and Caesar. Buddy Brown and Sandsablaze had only 8 faults (a foot in the water), and at the end of the first round, Mexico was 2½ points ahead of the United States. In a dramatic showdown in the second round of the competition, the Mexican crowds openly greeted the American riders with boos and hisses, while their own team members were cheered and applauded. Fernando Senderos of Mexico, riding Jet Run, a former U.S. jumper, had a clear round. While the American riders did incur faults, they nevertheless improved upon their performance in the first round sufficiently enough to win the team gold with 44¼ points, beating the Mexican team with 46½ and the Canadians with 76¾.

Senderos was the hero of the 1975 Games, winning the individual gold in jumping over Americans Buddy Brown and Michael Matz. However, with its clean sweep of team gold medals, the United States could consider the event a definite success. Buddy Brown and Michael Matz were joined by Melanie Smith and Norman dello Joio four years later to win the team gold in the 1979 Pan American Games, giving the American jumping team four victories out of the six Pan American Games at which it competed—a record to be proud of.

In the early days, the teams from South America appeared to have been much stronger than they are today. Questioned about this, Bertalan de Némethy points out that most of the successful riders were army officers who were simply not followed by riders with enough experience when they ceased to compete. He considers General Mariles of Mexico the most talented and also points to the high-jump record set by Chile. "They have good horses," he says, "especially the Thoroughbreds of Argentina, where racing is popular. Argentina also has some good riders, such as Dr. Hugo Arambide. But no one else comes along, and they are not well organized." He cites, as a similar example, the fact that America's Fort Riley, under the military, had all the necessary facilities, yet was not organized the same as the USET was later. Organization, he claims, is the key.

A PLACE OF HONOR

Under the coaching of de Némethy, the USET jumping team took its place among its neighbors to the south and surpassed them in the sport of show jumping. What is more, it maintained its composure and sportsmanlike behavior even under such adverse conditions as the distracting insults of the spectators at Mexico City in 1975. While South America had the resources—namely, the horse-breeding countries and military riders—necessary for competition, the United States was unique in its system of organizing and preparing its horses and riders through a nonmilitary instrument, the U.S. Equestrian Team.

Even Canada, a longtime rival on the North American fall show circuit, could not match the success of the Americans at the Pan American Games. The United States had achieved a place of honor in show jumping in the Western Hemisphere. As expressed by journalist Max Ammann in *The Chronicle of the Horse*, February 4, 1972, some weeks after the "probably worst showing of any American jumping team in any international championship (referring to the 1955 Pan American Games), Bert de Némethy was hired as coach of the USET Nations Cup Squad. Two and a half years later they were world class and still are."

6

De Némethy on Course Design

Over the decades, show jumping in the United States has seen enormous improvement in terms of horse and rider preparation and has progressed even more dramatically in knowledge of course design. The eight-fence, twice-around courses of the past have developed to the extent that even the smaller shows today offer what resemble "mini" Olympic courses that test the competitor at every level in new ways, with nothing left to chance.

Bertalan de Némethy was engaged as a course designer in 1954, when the Pan American Games trials were being held by the USET at Oak Brook, Illinois. By that time, Americans realized that they had to plan their courses along the lines of what they would encounter abroad. De Némethy's imaginative, impressive design captured the attention of riders and organizers alike and initiated preliminary discussion about how he might further benefit the USET, although he did not become officially affiliated with the Team until a year later.

Prior to the involvement of the USET, course design in America was primitive in comparison to that of Europe. Our progress has had a direct relationship to Team activities. Exposure to international competition abroad and the knowledge of cavalletti and gymnastic jumping offered by Bertalan de Némethy as coach led to development in this area. Different kinds of screening trials began to be held every third year at

THE DE NÉMETHY YEARS

William Steinkraus taking a water obstacle at Aachen. Prior to the involvement of the USET, course design in America was primitive in comparison with that of Europe. *Courtesy of the USET*

Gladstone and other locations throughout the country over European-type courses designed by de Némethy, and sophisticated courses grew out of his ideas and the inspiration provided by team experience in other countries.

Course design today is a complex blending of scientific principles and artistic imagination. De Némethy explains that the first responsibility of the course designer is to produce the best horse/rider combination possible. To achieve this, he must consider many things: the level and type of competition, the materials and show personnel that are available to him, construction and distances, variety, pleasing the spectators, and presenting an interesting challenge to the competitors that will inevitably be won by the best prepared horse and rider. It is more difficult, he notes, to design courses at the lower levels; they must be both accurate and inviting. Possibilities increase when one is planning for higher-level competition, but the end result should never be left to an element of luck.

"Courses are made according to the knowledge of the best riders and horses that have been produced," says de Némethy. In amateur classes, it is often possible for a less capable rider on a good horse to beat a good rider on a lesser horse; in other words, it is more difficult to produce the ideal combination. The best young horses with average riders will usually win.

The horse's experience is furthered by the use of a variety of obstacles, which should build confidence in young horses and offer challenges and interest to those at the higher levels. A good course designer, explains de Némethy, will plan an easy first class with few problems—more of a "schooling" course—and gradually introduce all the fences at his disposal. He should not take the competitors by surprise, but should build up to a final situation, such as a big money class or a last-day competition, for which the horses and riders have been gradually prepared. Essentially, courses should be appropriate, interesting, and safe.

On the latter subject, de Némethy estimates that 50 percent of the responsibility for a bad accident rests on the shoulders of the course designer, who must have the foresight and experience to allow for horses to "escape" from their mistakes uninjured. This requires an understanding of construction and close attention to detail. Rails must not sit too deeply in their cups; heavy, solid obstacles should be neither too wide nor too heavy to move in sections and should graduate in depth from the base of support, becoming narrower as they get higher; a heavy gate should be supported resting flat in the cups so that it can slide out safely; these and numerous other considerations must be well thought out in advance by the safety-conscious course designer. Poles should be a minimum of four inches around and should be matched at either end in order to be totally accurate. With this in mind, de Némethy had one end of each pole cut to match the other exactly when he planned the World Cup course in Baltimore in 1982.

Pleasing the spectators is another important consideration. De Némethy avoids the use of bright colors and startling designs, such as bull's-eyes, preferring a natural look and creating a pleasant effect by means of attractively coordinated natural colors and materials. "Riding is a natural thing," he emphasizes. "It should not be made artificial. It [course designing] is a little like the fashion business."

Common sense, knowledge, and experience are important in a good course designer, who combines the talents of mathematician, artist, and engineer in applying his skills. Possessing these qualities, de Némethy has helped maintain high standards for the United States.

WORLD CUP COURSE

Ironically, de Némethy was criticized by the foreign press and accused of designing his World Cup Final course in Baltimore in 1982 in such a way as to benefit the Americans. Those journalists who had expected victory from their nations' star equestrians had to place the blame somewhere when there was no success story to report, so they maintained that de Némethy's genius enabled him to design courses for Americans that the Europeans could not jump.

"Ridiculous!" declared de Némethy. When he reproduced and presented the plans for the Baltimore course at a 1982 course design seminar in Dublin, he pointed out that, in Baltimore, the Americans had placed first and second, fifth and sixth, and ninth and tenth. "But the next year," he quickly added, "we were in Birmingham, England, where I was only the technical delegate and was not designing any fences. What was the result? The Americans placed first and second, fifth and sixth, and ninth and tenth—different horses and different riders!"

A Swiss magazine conceded that the Americans proved they don't need an American course designer, but can do just as well anywhere.

His World Cup plans were well received and complimented at the European seminar. De Némethy explained that every fence used for the final competition had been used before and had been jumped in other ways. Distances also corresponded to previous parts of the competition. He told his fascinated audience, "I heard a couple of people complain about the striding on the water jump. If anyone needs more than 112 feet to jump the water, he shouldn't be there!" His remark met with laughter, but the point had been made.

De Némethy also explained that, in World Cup competition, you can ask much more than you usually would, as you are designing the course for the best in the world. The horses and riders have been consistently good over a period of time and should be ready for the challenge. An Olympic course is different, says de Némethy, because everyone who represents his country is not necessarily on top in comparison to the other nations of the world; not all countries produce jumpers of equal ability. On the other hand, it cannot be too easy, but must prompt the riders to think and to figure out the best ways in which to ride the course. To separate the good from the best, it is necessary to present some rider problems, as long as you are fair and know how far you can go in increasing the difficulty. De Némethy was complimented by the FEI, and his plans and comments were applauded at the seminar.

De Némethy believes that a good course designer should be familiar with riding courses and able to draw upon his own experience. "A good designer should be an experienced rider," he asserts. "He should know what is easy, difficult, possible, and impossible." Occasionally, there may be the exception—a knowledgeable person who has been able to learn through years of observation and can function in much the same way as a music critic who has never actually performed.

Left, Marcel Rozier, French chef d'equipe, and Bertalan de Némethy at the 1982 World Championships. *Courtesy Eastern Horse World/Bill Bohn*

This, however, is rare. Experience is the best qualification, according to de Némethy, when you are dealing with the top horses and riders, and strong riding judgment is an asset. "I can build courses because I rode them," he says.

COURSE DESIGN TODAY

Course designing today is an exacting profession. The course designer faces the individual problems of planning for several categories of jumper courses, including Preliminary, Intermediate, Open Jumper, and Amateur Owner. He must be highly imaginative in planning courses week after week without repeating himself excessively or, at the other extreme, making the courses too difficult.

Years ago, the responsibility of the course lay with the show manager, in addition to his numerous other duties. The result was that the courses were hastily set up, using a minimum of equipment and help in the way of ground crew. Consequently, the courses were so predictable that there was little challenge, prompting hurried preparation of horses for competition and even encouraging such crude practices as poling to hasten the progress of green jumpers. Measurements were haphazard, distances were "guesswork," and a clever horse could negotiate the course by throwing in an extra stride where needed. With today's high standards, nothing can be left to chance.

Says de Némethy, "The course designer runs the risk of making impossible courses when he is forced to stretch his imagination too much and repeat his courses every weekend. It is important to be different, yet there is a limit to the kinds and number of fences and variations. I remember what I did before and don't want to repeat it, but the equipment is always the same, supplied by the same few companies."

One solution would be to restrict the number of times that a show can employ the same course designer—perhaps no more than three times in a row. This, says de Némethy, might be controlled by the American Horse Shows Association. As the governing organization for American equestrian activities, the AHSA could have a list of accredited or licensed course designers in the rule book, impose a limit as to how many times they can design courses for the same shows, and encourage improvement through education. Course designers might be required, like judges, to attend seminars or to assist another course designer at two or three shows. Seminars have been held in recent years, de Némethy points out, but participation is optional and the right people—that is, the most promising course designers—do not necessarily attend. There are very few good course designers in the United States at present, claims de Némethy, estimating the number at six or seven. Since the AHSA sanctions the shows, he reasons, it should also have some influence on and control over the courses.

De Némethy believes that changes will eventually be made, although not overnight. "Unlike other countries," he observes, "the United States is slow to change." He would also like to see the same rules upheld all over the world rather than different national and international rules. "This is a problem with many sports," he comments.

One of the areas that has recently come under criticism in the United States is that of the junior equitation division, notably the Medal and Maclay finals. "Equitation is for style and should not have the problems of a Grand Prix course," says de Némethy. "An equitation course should show a fluid, forward, balanced ride." He likes to see equitation riders in balance and rhythm with their horses, without disturbing them, and this cannot be accomplished if they are beset by unusual problems, such as those of an advanced jumping course or a cross-country test. De Némethy is outspoken against artificial practices and will not officiate under such conditions.

He also cautions against making hunter courses too artificial. In recent years, he finds, hunter courses have departed, in many instances, from the natural concept and have begun to resemble jumper courses, with bright colors and stadium-type fences. This is something he regrets, and he urges a return to the more natural course, over suitable hunter obstacles and in an appropriate setting.

THE AMERICAN DIFFERENCE

In the past, according to de Némethy, our hunter and equitation courses have been responsible for both promoting good horses and horsemanship and providing good preparation for jumping competition. In this way, the American system differs greatly from that of the European countries, where there are as yet no such divisions. In Dublin in 1982, de Némethy found that the Europeans were impressed with our hunter and junior classes and expressed interest in holding similar ones at their own shows.

There are other differences between American and European horse shows that may directly or indirectly affect courses. For one thing, the great size and varied terrain of the United States provide additional considerations for both riders and course designers, who must be prepared for indoor or outdoor shows on either coast, in different climates and surroundings, with footing that may be dry or soggy, depending on the weather conditions. As de Némethy points out, in addition to having a top horse and being in good form, it is also necessary to have experience under all kinds of conditions.

Another difference is that, in the United States, show jumping is only one of many divisions of a typical horse show, rather than an exclusive competition as is usually the case in Europe. There are so many divisions of the American Horse Shows Association and so many specialized riding interests here, such as Western, saddle horse, hunters, breed competitions, and equitation, that show jumping locations and the number of classes offered are determined by many factors. The course designer has to consider the overall picture, as well as the basic components of a course, such as its line, spacing, distances, height and spread of obstacles, number of obstacles, time element, and so forth. His success lies in his ability to tie it all together into a neat "package" that will fairly test, yet challenge, the horses and riders and allow the best to emerge.

This was de Némethy's goal when he designed the courses for the Atlantic City International Equestrian Festival in December 1982. Since he was allowed to select the materials to be used in the course construction, he had enough variety to be able to present many of the same fences in different ways, so that horses and riders were introduced to almost every fence at some time during the show. He also added some new fences without changing the distances, thus preparing the competitors for the final effort by building them up to it earlier in the show. He tried to make the obstacles different but natural in appearance, explaining, "This is better than just making 'big' fences." The natural look is something he feels very strongly about. Recalling a blue wall that he saw in Dublin, de Némethy chuckles, "Did you ever see a blue wall?" The Atlantic City course was a new challenge that allowed him to stretch his imagination, but de Némethy laments the fact that there are too few people willing to accept such a challenge. "Why should I be the only one to come up with new ideas?" he wonders. "Everyone [interested in course design] should!"

De Némethy was pleased with the outcome, for he believes that his course was geared to the rider's intelligence and to the best schooled horses. Michael Matz and Honest Tom emerged as winners over Germany's Norbert Koof and Fire II, second, and Melanie Smith on Calypso, third. Matz exemplifies the "thinking" rider, who sometimes takes chances that pay off, and de Némethy felt that the results were just as they should have been. All three of the top-placing competitors in the Corinthian Grand Prix had already proven themselves as world champions. In allowing the best horse/rider combinations to win, de Némethy regarded his efforts as a success.

Winner Michael Matz comments, "The course was not very high, but there were a lot of rider problems. You needed a very careful horse for it." He agrees that de Némethy achieved his goal, adding that Norbert Koof and Melanie Smith were "good competition." Melanie Smith and Calypso had a clean round with a time of 30.71, which Koof and Fire II topped in 29.90. Michael Matz faced an almost impossible challenge, but Honest Tom's tight turns completed the course in 29.17 seconds for a $15,000 share of the purse.

De Némethy has demonstrated his expertise in course design, and his ideas will be a major factor at the 1984 Olympics. Course design today is a sophisticated skill, combining artistic imagination and scientific knowledge, and only a handful of individuals have managed to excel. Bertalan de Némethy ranks among the best.

THE DE NÉMETHY YEARS

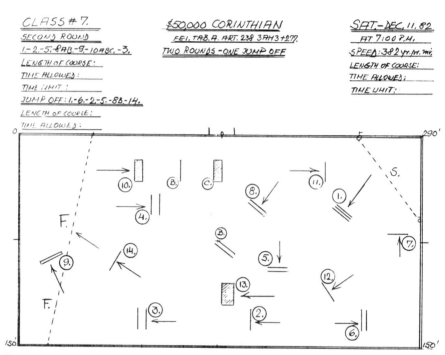

Course designs for the Atlantic City International Equestrian Festival, December 1982. As Michael Matz explained, "The course was not very high, but there were a lot of rider problems." De Némethy was satisfied with the outcome.

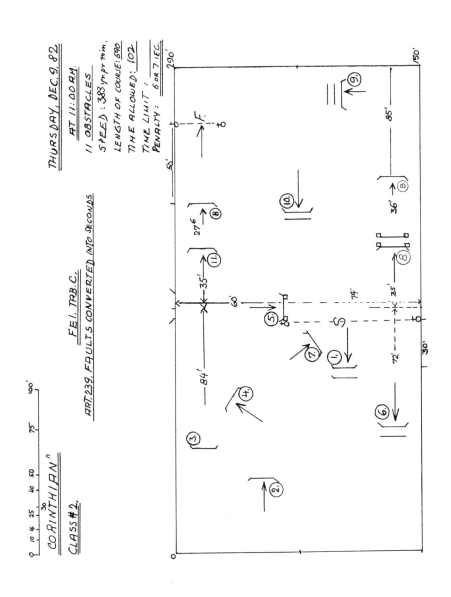

7

The de Némethy Touch in America

When Bertalan de Némethy first came to this country, the training of open jumpers reflected a depressing lack of knowledge of the principles of horsemanship, often resulting in some extreme practices.

As an example, consider the case of a young horse that becomes excited before a fence, and when the rider fights him, begins to rush and to anticipate the jump. Lacking control, the rider goes to a more severe bit. The horse then tries to escape the bit by raising his head, at which point the rider attaches a tight martingale. Pretty soon, the horse is such a bundle of nerves that he looks like a wind-up toy approaching a fence. This is the kind of situation that was not uncommon twenty-five or thirty years ago. Systematic schooling for jumpers was unknown—or at least not practiced—and jumper training was hasty and erratic.

Open jumpers were "second-class citizens" of the show ring who could not win in hunter classes, where conformation was even more important then than it is now. "Hunters had to be pleasant to ride," says de Némethy. "Because it was pleasant and elegant-looking, the best horse owners were interested only in the hunter division. Jumping was not as appealing." Since the hunter division and its requirements were already pretty clearly defined by the time de Némethy came upon the scene, his influence extended more to show jumping and its development.

Starting with the basics, de Némethy popularized modified dressage or "elementary training" for the schooling of jumpers. The word "dressage" met with suspicion in the early stages, and many people, including seasoned horsemen, associated it with circus tricks and the like. Today it is acknowledged that hunters and jumpers must follow signals, not resist, and be supple, obedient, and relaxed. In this respect, according to de Némethy, there is no line between hunters and jumpers. Today both are schooled according to the principles of elementary dressage.

In an interview for *Horse Play* (Bert: The de Némethy Touch in American Riding" by Paula Rodenas, October 1981), de Némethy stated: "A well-trained international jumper could go into Third Level dressage. He can do flying changes, work on two tracks, rein-backs and canter departures, and a quick turn on the haunches that I call the 'jumping pirouette,' which is almost a half pirouette."

Collection, as practiced in higher level dressage, can also be advantageous to the jumper, who must be capable of collecting (shortening) and lengthening in order to adjust to the course. "Before you can think of jumping," says de Némethy, "the horse must understand you. You must have control." He emphasizes the need for suppling exercises and takes pride in the fact that some of his jumpers have been able to perform extensions at the trot that made dressage aficionados sit up and take notice. His emphasis on flat work and the basic principles of horsemanship are results of de Némethy's own classical riding education. "In the art of riding," he has been heard to say many times, "there have been no changes for centuries." The goal of training is to teach the horse to maintain his balance even under the added weight of the rider; to develop and maintain the proper rhythm; to improve the horse's coordination; to condition through the right kind of daily exercise; to instill confidence in the horse; and to teach the horse to understand and respond to the aids of the rider. None of this theory is new; it is simply that de

THE DE NÉMETHY TOUCH IN AMERICA

Lungeing has many benefits, according to de Némethy, shown here with Royal Duke at Stonyhill. *Photograph by the author*

Némethy has employed it systematically, to its highest degree, in the preparation of his jumpers.

LUNGEING

Lungeing has played an important role in the development of de Némethy's horses and riders. Before every Olympic Games, with the exception of Montreal, he leased horses for the purpose of lungeing the riders prior to competition. Many were lunged in a dressage seat, without stirrups, for half an hour every day before going into the arena, including William Steinkraus before winning his gold medal at Mexico City in 1968. The benefits to the rider can be summed up in one short phrase: teaching him to sit on the horse.

Lungeing is, in the words of de Némethy, "an art." It teaches the horse to carry himself properly, puts him in a frame, and improves his coordination and his response to aids just as in mounted schooling. The lunge line and whip replace the rider's legs. "It must be done correctly and with the right equipment," cautions de Némethy. "Too few have the patience to do this." He is critical of the "lazy way" of lungeing the horse in a halter instead of under tack, as a means of exercise rather than schooling. Horses are affected by everything a rider does, and the benefits of lungeing, when done correctly, make it worth the effort of doing it the de Némethy way.

CAVALLETTI

Another good example of the de Némethy touch is his use of cavalletti. Although cavalletti started in Italy with Caprilli, de Némethy was the person who turned their use into an art and combined them with gymnastic jumping exercises to prepare horses and riders for jumping. "I am not claiming to have invented the cavalletti," he explained in the *Horse Play* interview. "On the other hand, I do claim to have invented the way they are used here." His methods arose from need, as illustrated by the five weeks in which he had to ready his horses and riders for the Olympic tryouts back in 1955. The system worked so well that it became a standard part of de Némethy's training methods and can be observed working its magic in his clinics today.

Today almost every backyard stable has cavalletti. "I have studied many books," says de Némethy, "but I have never found any rules for cavalletti or gymnastic work." He adds, "It depends upon common sense—adjusting yourself to the rider's and horse's ability and stage of training and using enough imagination to realize what they need to be improved."

THE DE NÉMETHY TOUCH IN AMERICA

The use of cavalletti is an important part of the de Némethy method. Gina Morin demonstrates at a Stonyhill clinic riding True Mahogany. *Photograph by Kenneth Rodenas*

The benefits of cavalletti are many. Cavalletti work improves the horse's jumping ability by developing his coordination, suppleness, and concentration. It also serves as an exercise in timing for the rider. A rider obviously cannot practice over hundreds of jumps every day, but, as de Némethy points out, each time you use cavalletti you are learning to jump.

The cavalletti work gives the rider what de Némethy calls a "slow motion" kind of analysis or awareness of rhythm, impulsion, connection with the horse's mouth, and position of his own upper body. "As long as you know what you're doing and have self-discipline, concentration, and control, the horse and rider can improve together," says de Némethy. He believes that almost every horse and rider can be improved, but adds,

"Without personal ability, one can only get to a certain level." The rider develops his eye for distance, as well as his balance, sense of timing, and control of the horse prior to take-off and learns to be in harmony with his mount at the critical take-off point, when he must be careful not to interfere. Since there are no existing written rules, de Némethy's experience and knowledge have determined the use of cavalletti and gymnastic exercises. He knows instinctively how far he can push each horse and rider. His methods have enabled him to obtain relatively quick results without sacrificing quality or ignoring the classical principles that he so carefully upholds.

INTERNATIONAL EXPOSURE

Exposure to international competition has been highly important in the development of American riders, affecting both course design and an awareness of how Americans measure up against the other equestrian nations of the world. "I was very successful," admits de Némethy, "in selling my executive committee—mostly supported by Whitney Stone—on the idea that we cannot stay in this country and make progress." He urged the committee, "We have to compete against the best in the world and go to many different places to find out whether we are good or bad. If we stay at the same shows—Gladstone and Devon and Ox Ridge—we wind up beating each other. By traveling to Europe, we realize that we are good, but others are better, because they are beating us!"

More and more Americans, including riders and horse owners, took heed and began to go to the Olympics and other international events and to make comparisons. "Very few went to Amsterdam in 1920," de Némethy notes, "but in Tokyo, Mexico City, and Munich, there were hundreds of American equestrian people. The more we went to Europe, the more we improved."

As a result of this international exposure, even today's small shows have jumping courses that are sophisticated and far better in design than those of twenty-five years ago. As one horseman says, the amateur owner and junior jumper courses of today look like modified versions of Olympic courses. Show jumping in America has a much larger number of good horses and riders than ever before, and its standards are high.

THE "IMAGE"

An important side effect of the de Némethy touch in connection with international exposure is the "image" he has created. The "cowboy" association with American riding vanished as Team members exhibited great style in their attire, turnout, performance, and manner, maintaining morale and discipline wherever they went. They were impressive not only in their riding, but in their behavior as well, with no signs of personal conflicts or rebellion. The other nations were astounded and their praises were sung at home. Parents began to view riding as a positive influence on their youngsters. As de Némethy points out, riders are tired after riding six or seven horses a day and have no time for anything else. Furthermore, the sport demands discipline of mind and body.

Bertalan de Némethy has set a fine example for trainers and instructors in the United States. His innovative use of cavalletti, dressage, and lungeing techniques are accepted practices among many leading professionals, who, in turn, are responsible for improving the caliber of horsemanship in the United States, especially among the junior riders. De Némethy's logical progression of lungeing, elementary schooling, cavalletti, and gymnastic jumping has been adopted by others in the interest of building the horse's physique and confidence while improving the abilities of the rider. The system is not impersonal, but as de Némethy has demonstrated, can meet individual requirements.

The application of historical concepts, accomplished with a singular touch of brilliance, is what initially set de Némethy apart and enabled him to make significant contributions to American riding. While not an "inventor," he has certainly been a leader. De Némethy was not the first European to bring his ideas to America, but was unique in his means of communicating and applying his ideas. The force of his convictions, his magnetic personality, and his quest for perfection have made him outstanding in his field; it is through his personality that he has so successfully made his influence felt. Inspired by the positive criticism and examples set by his own cavalry teachers, de Némethy has been able to understand the feelings of his riders and to deal with them individually. "A coach cannot afford to make too many mistakes," he says. "He must be consistent in his judgment." In this, he has been successful.

De Némethy's quest for perfection influenced individual Team members and consequently set an example for the rest of the country. In addition to being a role model, the USET, inspired by William Steinkraus's initial idea, took an important step toward promoting horsemanship for young riders in 1965 by instating an advanced equitation division to fill the gap for those who had qualified for the Medal/Maclay finals. The USET class was intended to provide incentive and additional experience prior to the National Horse Show, after the riders had qualified for the other finals and had thereby become ineligible for further competition.

Today the United States Equestrian Team Medal Finals are held on the East and West coasts in the fall of the year. The competition begins with equitation on the flat, followed by gymnastics, where the riders are judged over three different series of gymnastic lines. In the third phase, they negotiate a course of at least ten fences 3 feet 6 inches to 3 feet 9 inches high with spreads to 5 feet 0 inches (excluding a water jump of 8 feet with a pole over it) and including a double and triple combination, with at least one spread fence in each. The four top riders, selected by the judges for their form and execution, go on to jump a round on each of the four horses that have qualified for the final ride-off. The champion is the competitor who has demonstrated superior capabilities throughout the four phases. The winners of the two finals competitions are invited to participate in an official USET training session, and special trophies are presented to their trainers. While Steinkraus cites de Némethy as a good example of what a horseman should be, the Team likewise establishes goals for the young rider and provides further encouragement through high standards of competition.

THE DE NÉMETHY INFLUENCE

William Steinkraus cites de Némethy's imagination, idealism, knowledge, training, and riding ability as the ingredients that were obviously important to the Team at a time when different training strategy was needed. In 1952, he recalls, Team members felt they were ten or fifteen years behind the Europeans in the evolution of the sport as practiced on the Continent. De Némethy was in the right place at the right time and absolutely able to meet the challenge. He also had the good fortune to encounter other dedicated horsemen and the equine resources and jumping potential of the American Thoroughbred. He was able to create a little cavalry school at Gladstone, which, at that time, was the only place for serious amateurs. Turning professional today is more attractive than it was ten years ago, according to Steinkraus, who felt a strong commitment during the 1950's and 1960's, when the USET had a big investment in its riders. Steinkraus could have retired in 1968 but preferred to wait until other good young riders came along —until he felt he was no longer essential. By the same token, his philosophy is that nobody is truly indispensable. The United States' preconditioning to having competitive teams is so strong that even a major disaster would not prevent us from having a team to compete in the Olympics. Had de Némethy not appeared on the scene, the Team would have had to find someone else, and quickly, says Steinkraus—probably another European, but certainly not another Bert de Némethy, whose role could not have been filled in the same way by anyone else. As Steinkraus puts it, "Nobody else could be a Bert de Némethy as well as Bert de Némethy."

THE DE NÉMETHY YEARS

Chrystine Jones and Ksarina

Dennis Murphy and Tuscaloosa

Throughout de Némethy's 25 years as coach and beyond, the USET jumping team has remained a source of pride to America. *Courtesy of the USET*

Mary Mairs and Tomboy

Carol Hofmann and Salem

THE DE NÉMETHY YEARS

Joe Fargis and Bonte II

Frank Chapot and White Lightning

THE DE NÉMETHY TOUCH IN AMERICA

Kathy Kusner and Triple Crown

Robert Ridland and Almost Persuaded

THE DE NÉMETHY YEARS

The success of the American riders has had an impact upon the rest of the world. During the 1960's, the Germans were forced to reevaluate their attitude as the Americans started to beat them at their own game. They also took note of the American Thoroughbred, and many turned to a lighter type of competition horse. Douglas Bunn, who created the All-England Jumping Course at Hickstead, remarked in the *USET Book of Riding* that the USET had set a standard for show jumpers in Europe and inspired improvement in the sport during the 1950's under de Némethy's influence. Thus the de Némethy touch extended even beyond national boundaries.

It is in the United States, however, that we can observe the most dramatic changes. In the past twenty-five or thirty years, American riding has progressed from undisciplined training methods and the use of gadgetry to a new appreciation of classical truths. The contributions of Bertalan de Némethy were an important factor in helping to bring about this revolution and made a profound impression.

8
Looking Ahead

"Humans have a tremendous urge to do a little bit more and a little bit better than before," observes Bertalan de Némethy. "Thus the requirements are made more difficult. This is true of every sport."

As far as show jumping is concerned, he predicts, "In our lifetime, very few horses will go over eight feet, unless, perhaps, they have been especially bred for this purpose."

Records have been set by Chile (2 meters 47 centimeters) and Italy (2 meters 45 centimeters), both equivalent to over eight feet. But progress of this nature is limited, since the most important concept of course design is not to injure horses or create potentially dangerous situations, but to separate experienced riders and well-trained horses from those who are less prepared, by means of imagination, an understanding of riding problems, knowing what is possible and what is fair, and promoting harmony between horse and rider so that the best combination will win. These considerations are directed toward improving the sport in terms of producing better horses and riders rather than seeking the rare exceptions. Progress will be determined by furthering our knowledge of course design, systematically training horses and riders, and perhaps by efforts on the part of breeders, who strive to obtain superior sporting horses.

THE SPORT TODAY

Today we see more professionals on the scene, as mentioned earlier, because the average amateur does not have sufficient time and money to fully pursue the sport. Sponsorships are becoming increasingly important. Corporations such as Rolex, Insilco, Almaden Vineyards, and others have added their support to equestrian sports in recent years (equestrian competition was formerly overlooked in favor of other, more popular spectator sports such as baseball, football, basketball, golf, and tennis). Sponsors provide money, which in turn provides more competition for the generous prizes. However, as de Némethy cautions, this means that the average horse and rider may not be able to measure up. Only the best will make it as show jumping becomes more of a spectator sport and more demanding.

The amounts of prize money continue to grow. For example, at Valley Forge in 1982, $25,000 worth of prize money was offered. As the purses grow, competition becomes more keen.

The United States has no tradition regarding the televising of equestrian events, unlike Europe, where equestrian figures are as well known to viewers as baseball players are in the United States. Only racing has been widely televised here. Spectators have not been educated to appreciate equestrian competition. Sponsors are influenced by TV ratings, whereas in many European countries, there is little or no commercial TV. Equestrian sports cannot vie with the more popular national sports that are currently televised, and unless viewers speak up, the situation will remain the same.

"It will be slow to change," agrees de Némethy, although he feels there has been some improvement in the last twenty-five years with the advent of cable television. Perhaps in cable TV lie our hopes for the promotion of equestrian activities as spectator sports.

Dressage is yet to be appreciated by the average layman, but eventing has gained interest because of the participation of international figures such as Princess Anne and Captain

The 1982 show jumping team at the World Championships, *left to right*, Michael Matz on Jet Run, Bernie Traurig on Eadenvale, Peter Leone on Ardennes, and Melanie Smith on Calypso. *Courtesy Eastern Horse World/Bill Bohm*

Mark Phillips. The Rolex Kentucky Horse Trials have received good media coverage—at least locally—and viewers find the cross-country exciting. Show jumping has been televised more and more on cable TV, including portions of the National Horse Show. While much has been filmed of Olympic and other international competition, however, only a few minutes actually get on the air, mainly as part of news broadcasts or special sports programs. It is to be hoped that this will change as our equestrians continue to perform well, viewers become more involved, and corporate sponsors keep adding their support.

PROGRESS IN AMERICA

The progress of riding in America has been noticed by people such as de Némethy, who are able to look back over a relatively long period and compare. As de Némethy stated in *Horse Play* in October 1981, "During the last twenty-five years, in every discipline, riding has improved and developed in the United States. In jumping and three-day, we are one of the strongest nations in the world."

Noting the changing dressage picture, he added, "It is interesting that in many countries so traditionally associated with dressage, such as Germany and Sweden, . . . there are not as many top German and Swedish dressage riders. In Switzerland, there is only one woman (Christine Stueckelberger). Where are the French? Their traditions and facilities still exist, supported by the government, but they cannot produce a dressage team at the Olympics.

"We seem to be a little impatient with dressage," he continues. "The good-hearted Americans at first bought horses from Germany that nobody else wanted to ride. Now they are clever and cannot be fooled any more. We're still not on top in dressage, but it's coming."

THE JUNIOR COMPETITORS

Today's juniors represent the future of American riding, and it is the equitation division that must be carefully watched. Hugh Wiley, who teaches and trains nationally, says, "This is a bad time for riding, because the majority are pushing aside de Némethy's way for the 'quick fix' sort of thing, where the rider sits prettily and does nothing on an expensive horse. 'Equitation' is becoming a 'dirty' word." Many people today are teaching a two-point position with a stiff back, he finds, and are unable to teach de Némethy's way because they do not understand it. The judges, he notes, are pinning riders who do not use the aids properly. There is hope, however, that the truth will dawn on those who aspire to advance. As Wiley points out, "Not many can jump six-foot fences or ride a Grand Prix course. To do this, they must ride like de Némethy teaches. There are many 'gimmicky' trainers, but it all comes back to de Némethy." Many former equitation riders, such as Conrad Homfeld and Katie Monahan, he adds, have risen above the equitation situation.

"De Némethy's methods are superior to anyone else's," concludes Wiley. "He is recognized as a master in stadium jumping. His method is relaxed and simple and flows with the movement of the horse."

One former Team member who has departed from the cavalletti system as used by de Némethy is George Morris, who teaches hunt seat equitation and has brought more juniors along than anyone else in recent years. Cavalletti is a part of his training, but it is used in odd places as a "stabilizer," more in the manner of Littauer, while the crossrail becomes more important and is used in repetition to establish correct habits in the rider. Morris recognizes cavalletti as a good exercise but, unlike de Némethy, does not consider it the "meat and potatoes" of his training. "I am part Bert and part other things," he explains. Morris advocates the crest release for beginners or intermediate riders because it ensures that the horse will not be hit in the mouth. The out-of-hand release, he feels, is not practical at the lower

THE DE NÉMETHY YEARS

Hugh Wiley practicing with Master William in earlier years. "De Némethy's methods are superior to anyone else's," concludes Wiley. *Courtesy of the USET*

level. "All the releases have their merits," he says, pointing out that he is dealing with a wider range of riders than de Némethy, who works with the very best. Today's problems differ from those of the early years, when de Némethy had to shape the riding resources of a raw country into position and was, as Morris puts it, "the only game in town." Now there are many more trainers, owners, and stables, as well as a

Former Team rider George Morris is now a leading trainer whose young students take numerous national equitation honors. *Courtesy of Darkroom on Wheels*

greater number of riders on the scene, providing more variety in the approach to competitive riding.

THE FUTURE

The future, as George Morris sees it, is as yet unpredictable. We have more riders and schooled horses with which to work, but where we go from here, he feels, depends largely upon our ability to organize and channel our efforts.

There are some who believe that rule changes will occur in show jumping. Frank Chapot, for example, feels that the AHSA and FEI rules will come closer together. "There are good and bad parts of the FEI rules," he says. "I think we'll discard the bad and keep the good."

In terms of international competitors, de Némethy feels that although the United States and Germany remain strong, the French and the Swiss have moved up rapidly in recent years. Both were good competitors at the 1982 National Horse Show, where the title of Leading Foreign International Rider went to France's Michel Robert. There was a three-way tie to win the Puissance between Rodney Jenkins and Arbitrage of the United States, Michel Robert and Venus de Ver of France, and Walter Gabathuler and Beethoven II of Switzerland, all clearing the wall at a reported record height for Madison Square Garden of 7 feet 6 inches.

With today's USET organized differently than it was in the early years, de Némethy finds it difficult to predict where it will be five or ten years hence. Today there are more professionals competing and "doing their own thing," and consequently less control. In the early days, individual riders did not go alone to Europe; now they do not hesitate. De Némethy emphasizes the importance of strict organization. He points to France as an example, citing that the French, for many years, had leading breeders, good government support, and fine traditions, such as that of Saumur, the French national equestrian center. During the last fifteen years, they lost momentum, he says, but in the next five years, they will again be on top because of good leadership and organization and government support.

De Némethy continues to maintain that one of our best assets is the American Thoroughbred. "Many horses are

Rodney Jenkins and Arbitrage of the United States tied with Walter Gabathuler and Beethoven II of Switzerland and Michel Robert and Janus de Ver of France to clear the Puissance wall at 7 feet 6 inches at the 1982 National Horse Show. *Courtesy Eastern Horse World/Bill Bohn*

brought from Holland, Sweden, and other countries," he says, "but the American Thoroughbred is better." It may be harder to find the good ones, he adds, because America is such a big country, as compared to The Netherlands, for example, where almost every horse and every breeder are known because they live within a relatively small area. When a good horse comes along, declares de Némethy, everyone wants his brother! The success of the Dutch-bred Calypso and the Canadian-bred Windsor Castle were followed by frantic searches for related horses.

European horses are popular in the United States today and sell at auction for prices reaching upwards of $65,000. Yet, claims de Némethy, "A sound young Thoroughbred is just as capable as a European horse." There are exceptional horses of any type, he adds, mentioning the success the Germans have had with their warmbloods and the Italians with their Irish imports. And, of course, who can forget Stroller, that wonderful little jumper of Great Britain, who was only a pony? But, according to de Némethy, we should concentrate on the good horseflesh that is available to us in this country and not allow ourselves to become susceptible to fads.

In recent years, riders who come to the Team already prepared and who do not wish to change their styles have nonetheless felt the influence of de Némethy. Melanie Smith was a member of the last Nations Cup team coached by de Némethy before his retirement, competing on the 1980 summer circuit and at the National Horse Show. This 1982 winner of the Whitney Stone Memorial Cup presented by the USET for her achievement in competition and her international "ambassadorship" was very impressed with how well organized he was and found traveling with him a delight. "He spoke several languages and knew everybody," she remembers. Melanie came to the Team from a background of Pony Club and show riding and did not experience the intensive training sessions of the earlier days, when de Némethy was more of a coordinator. Melanie foresees a "modified return to the original system" as indicated by a ten-day training session directed by Frank Chapot prior to the 1983 Pan American Games. In spite of the discontinued long training sessions of the past, she feels there will be more of a group effort and feeling of team spirit that will reflect the traditions established by de Némethy.

Katie Monahan, American Grandprix Association Woman Rider of the Year in 1982, echoes Melanie Smith's enthusiasm for de Némethy's ability to organize. "Anything he did, he tried to do to perfection," she recalls. Even his way of holding the lunge line and whip when lungeing a horse is, to her, special. Katie rode with the Team in Europe in 1980 and, like Melanie, went to Gladstone only about a week or ten days before departure. Katie, however, had the opportunity of working with de Némethy on various occasions and watching him ride. She was especially impressed with his flat work because her own background did not include a heavy dressage influence. "That's when I really became aware of dressage," she says.

According to Katie Monahan, today's juniors are even more aware of the importance of dressage and proper schooling than she was. The courses today are difficult and demanding, and careful training is necessary to get a horse to Grand Prix level.

Reflecting on the Team in recent years, Katie summarizes: "In the past eight to ten years, there has not been a need for just one coach. Bert's role has changed. But no matter where the Team goes, it is very much respected."

Fellow competitor Michael Matz agrees that people such as William Steinkraus, Frank Chapot, and, indeed, de Némethy himself, are still teaching, spreading their influence, and affecting Team activities. "Bert's influence is still felt and will continue," he says. "The Team has a classic style that will go on in the future."

Chrystine Jones foresees an optimistic future for American show jumping, pointing to our record in the Pan American Games, Olympics, and World Championships. She notes that the development of Grand Prix show jumping in our country has had a decided effect, providing us with more prize money,

THE DE NÉMETHY YEARS

Melanie Smith (on Calypso) and Michael Matz (on Jet Run) are two riders of recent years who see a continuation of the de Némethy influence. *Courtesy Eastern Horse World/Bill Bohn*

LOOKING AHEAD

Chrystine Jones, Director of Show Jumping Activities for the USET, receiving the Hermès Trophy in 1982 from Patrick Guerrand-Hermès. *Courtesy of Miller's*

sponsors, horses, riders, and trainers than ever before. "Fund raising will be the big challenge of the eighties," she believes. Summarizing our position among the equestrian nations of the world, she concludes, "We are always a contender."

According to William Steinkraus, Bertalan de Némethy's place in equestrian history is secure. "You couldn't erase the traditions if you tried," he says. "They are part of our collective experience." He points out that even if thirty years from now, people ask, "Who was Bertalan de Némethy?", they will still be doing things his way, or at least in a later evolutionary stage.

On a more personal note, he believes that de Némethy has changed and grown during his years in the United States and that today he is comfortable with his life and capable of being happy with his vast experience now partly behind him. De Némethy's ability to "shift gears," in spite of the apparent inflexibility of his idealistic nature, serves as yet another inspiration.

The traditions established by the formation of the United States Equestrian Team and the contributions of Bertalan de Némethy have set the stage for the future. As long as American equestrians continue to seek improvement and observe high standards, the de Némethy years will not denote the close of an era, but will go on indefinitely.

Appendix
Major USET Jumping Victories
1956-1980

OLYMPIC AND PAN AMERICAN GAMES RESULTS

1956	Olympic Games Stockholm, Sweden	Hugh Wiley/ Trail Guide	11th
		William Steinkraus/ Night Owl	15th
		Frank Chapot/Belair	27th
		Team: 5th place	

1959	Pan American Games
	Chicago, U.S.A.
		Frank Chapot/Diamant
		Hugh Wiley/Nautical
		William Steinkraus/
		   Riviera Wonder
		George Morris/Night Owl
		No individual competition;
		   team: 1st place
		   (gold medal)	

1960	Olympic Games Rome, Italy	George Morris/Sinjon	4th
		Hugh Wiley/Master William	7th
		William Steinkraus/ Riviera Wonder	15th

Results courtesy of the United States Equestrian Team.

THE DE NÉMETHY YEARS

1960		Team: 2nd place (silver medal) (George Morris/Sinjon; Frank Chapot/Trail Guide; W. Steinkraus/Ksar d'Esprit)	
1963	Pan American Games São Paulo, Brazil	Mary Mairs/Tomboy	1st
		Frank Chapot/San Lucas	4th
		Kathy Kusner/Unusual	15th
		William Steinkraus/ Sinjon	ret.
		Team: 1st place (gold medal)	
1964	Olympic Games Tokyo, Japan	Frank Chapot/San Lucas	7th
		Kathy Kusner/ Untouchable	13th
		Mary Mairs/Tomboy	33rd
		Team: 6th place	
1967	Pan American Games Winnipeg, Canada	Kathy Kusner/ Untouchable	5th
		Mary Chapot/White Lightning	7th
		Frank Chapot/San Lucas	7th
		William Steinkraus/ Bold Minstrel	9th
		Team: 2nd place (silver medal)	
1968	Olympic Games Mexico City, Mexico	William Steinkraus/ Snowbound	1st
		Frank Chapot/San Lucas	4th
		Kathy Kusner/ Untouchable	21st

APPENDIX—MAJOR USET VICTORIES

1968		Team: 4th place (Mary Chapot/White Lightning; Kathy Kusner/Untouchable; Frank Chapot/San Lucas)	
1972	Olympic Games Munich, West Germany	Neal Shapiro/Sloopy	3rd
		Kathy Kusner/Fleet Apple	10th
		William Steinkraus/ Snowbound	22nd
		Team: 2nd place (silver medal) (Neal Shapiro/Sloopy; Kathy Kusner/Fleet Apple; Frank Chapot/ White Lightning; William Steinkraus/ Main Spring)	
1975	Pan American Games Mexico City, Mexico	Buddy Brown/A Little Bit	2nd
		Michael Matz/Grande	3rd
		Dennis Murphy/Do Right	7th
		Team: 1st place (gold medal) (Michael Matz/Grande; Dennis Murphy/Do Right; Joseph Fargis/ Caesar; Buddy Brown/ Sandsablaze)	
1976	Olympic Games Montreal, Canada	Frank D. Chapot/ Viscount	5th tied

147

THE DE NÉMETHY YEARS

1976		Dennis Murphy/Do Right	22nd
		Buddy Brown/A Little Bit	29th
		Team Competition	4th
		Buddy Brown/Sandsablaze Robert Ridland/ Southside Michael Matz/ Grande Frank Chapot/ Viscount	
1979	Pan American Games Puerto Rico	Michael Matz/Jet Run	1st
		Melanie Smith/Val de Loire	5th
		Team Competition:	1st
		Buddy Brown/Sandsablaze Norman Dello Joio/ Allegro Michael Matz/ Jet Run Melanie Smith/ Val de Loire	

APPENDIX—MAJOR USET VICTORIES

WORLD AND EUROPEAN CHAMPIONSHIP RESULTS

1956	Aachen World Championships	William Steinkraus/First Boy and Night Owl	5th
		Hugh Wiley/Master William	9th
1958	Aachen European Championships	William Steinkraus/ Ksar d'Esprit	5th
		Hugh Wiley/Nautical	6th
1959	Paris European Championships	William Steinkraus/First Boy and Ksar d'Esprit	5th
		Hugh Wiley/Nautical and Master William	6th
1960	Venice World Championships	William Steinkraus/ Ksar d'Esprit	4th
		George Morris/Sinjon	10th
1961	Aachen European Championships	Warren Wofford/ Hollandia and Huntsman	unpl.
1965	Hickstead Ladies' World Championships	Kathy Kusner/ Untouchable and That's Right	2nd
1966	Lucerne European Championships	Frank Chapot/Good Twist and San Lucas	2nd
		William Steinkraus/ Snowbound and Sinjon	withdrew
1967	Fontainebleau Ladies' European Championships	Kathy Kusner/ Untouchable and Aberali	1st

149

THE DE NÉMETHY YEARS

1970	La Baule World Championships	Frank Chapot/White Lightning	6th
		William Steinkraus/ Bold Minstrel	9th
1974	La Baule Ladies' World Championships	Michele McEvoy/Mr. Muskie and Sundancer	2nd
1974	Hickstead World Championships	Frank Chapot/Main Spring	3rd
		Rodney Jenkins/Idle Dice	8th
1978	Aachen World Championships	Michael Matz/Jet Run	3rd
		Conrad Homfeld/ Balbuco	12th
		Team: Matz, Homfeld, Dennis Murphy on Tuscaloosa, and Buddy Brown on Viscount	3rd

APPENDIX—MAJOR USET VICTORIES

NATIONS CUP RESULTS

1955	London	4th to Italy, Great Britain and Ireland
	Dublin	5th to Italy, Great Britain, Ireland and Sweden
	Le Zoute	4th to France, Great Britain and Belgium
	Harrisburg	4th to Ireland, Mexico and Canada
	New York	3rd to Mexico and Ireland
	Toronto	2nd to Ireland
1956	Stockholm	6th to Great Britain, Italy, Portugal, Spain and West Germany
	Aachen	5th to Brazil, West Germany, Spain and Portugal
	London	5th to Great Britain, Brazil, Turkey and Ireland
	Dublin	4th to Great Britain, Turkey and Ireland
	Harrisburg	2nd to Canada
	New York	4th to Mexico, Ireland and Canada
	Toronto	1st (Chapot/Defense; Wiley/Nautical; Steinkraus/First Boy)
1957	Harrisburg	2nd to Great Britain
	New York	1st (Chapot/Pill Box; Steinkraus/First Boy; Wiley/Nautical)
	Toronto	1st (Dennehy/Pill Box; Steinkraus/Night Owl; Wiley/Nautical)
1958	Aachen	2nd to Spain
	London	1st (Morris/Night Owl; Chapot/Diamant; Wiley/Nautical; Steinkraus/Ksar d'Esprit)
	Dublin	2nd to Great Britain
	Ostend	2nd to France
	Rotterdam	4th to France, West Germany and Ireland

151

1958	Harrisburg	3rd to West Germany and Canada
	New York	2nd to West Germany
	Toronto	3rd to West Germany and Canada
1959	Rome	1st (Morris/Sinjon; Chapot/Diamant; Steinkraus/Ksar d'Esprit; Wiley/Nautical)
	Paris	3rd to Soviet Union and West Germany
	Aachen	2nd to Italy
	London	1st (Morris/Night Owl; Chapot/Tally Ho; Steinkraus/Riviera Wonder; Wiley/Nautical)
	Harrisburg	1st (Morris/Sinjon; Chapot/Spring Board; Steinkraus/Trail Guide)
	New York	2nd to Canada
	Toronto	1st (Morris/Sinjon; Chapot/Spring Board; Steinkraus/Trail Guide)
1960	Lucerne	1st (Morris/Sinjon; Chapot/Tally Ho; Wiley/Nautical; Steinkraus/Riviera Wonder)
	Aachen	2nd to West Germany
	London	1st (Morris/Sinjon; Chapot/Tally Ho; Wiley/Master William; Steinkraus/Riviera Wonder)
	Ostend	2nd to France
	Harrisburg	2nd to Venezuela
	New York	2nd to Mexico
	Toronto	1st (Morris/Sinjon; Chapot/Ksar d'Esprit; Wiley/Master William)
1961	Harrisburg	1st (Chapot/Night Owl; Kusner/Sinjon; Steinkraus/Ksar d'Esprit)
	New York	elim (winner Argentina)
	Toronto	1st (Chapot/San Lucas; Kusner/Sinjon; Steinkraus/Ksar d'Esprit)

APPENDIX—MAJOR USET VICTORIES

1962 Aachen 1st (Robertson/The Sheriff; Mairs/Tomboy; Chapot/San Lucas; Steinkraus/Sinjon)

London 2nd to West Germany

Dublin 2nd to Italy

Harrisburg 1st (Mairs/Tomboy; Chapot/San Lucas; Steinkraus/Sinjon)

New York 1st (Mairs/Tomboy; Chapot/San Lucas; Steinkraus/Sinjon)

Toronto 1st (Mairs/Tomboy; Chapot/San Lucas; Robertson/Master William)

1963 Harrisburg 1st (Mairs/Tomboy; Chapot/Manon; Steinkraus/Fire One)

New York 1st (Mairs/Tomboy; Chapot/San Lucas; Steinkraus/Sinjon)

Toronto 1st (Mairs/Tomboy; Chapot/San Lucas; Steinkraus/Unusual)

1964 London 3rd to Great Britain and Italy

Dublin 1st (Mairs/Tomboy; Kusner/Untouchable; Chapot/Manon; Steinkraus/Sinjon)

Ostend 1st (Kusner/Untouchable; Hofmann/San Pedro; Chapot/San Lucas; Steinkraus/Sinjon)

Rotterdam 2nd to West Germany

New York 1st (Chapot/Manon; Kusner/Untouchable; Steinkraus/Sinjon; Shapiro/Jacks or Better)

Toronto 1st (Mairs/Tomboy; Kusner/Untouchable; Steinkraus/Sinjon)

1965 Harrisburg 1st (Mary Chapot/Tomboy; Kusner/Untouchable; Chapot/San Lucas; Steinkraus/Snowbound)

153

THE DE NÉMETHY YEARS

1965	New York	1st (Mary Chapot/Tomboy; Kusner/ Fire One; Chapot/San Lucas; Steinkraus/Sinjon)
	Toronto	1st (Hofmann/San Pedro; Kusner/ Unusual; Mary Chapot/Tomboy; Chapot/San Lucas)
1966	Lucerne	1st (Mary Chapot/Tomboy; Kusner/ Untouchable; Chapot/San Lucas; Steinkraus/Sinjon)
	Aachen	2nd to Italy
	Harrisburg	1st (Mary Chapot/Tomboy; Jones/ Fru; Chapot/San Lucas; Steinkraus/Snowbound)
	New York	1st (Mary Chapot/Tomboy; Steinkraus/Bold Minstrel; Chapot/ San Lucas; Kusner/Untouchable)
	Toronto	2nd to Canada
1967	Aachen	3rd to Great Britain and Italy
	New York	1st (Shapiro/Night Spree; Hofmann/ Salem; Kusner/Untouchable; Steinkraus/Snowbound)
	Toronto	1st (Jones/Trick Track; Shapiro/ Night Spree; Mary Chapot/ Anakonda; Kusner/Untouchable)
1968	London	1st (Mary Chapot/White Lightning; Kusner/Untouchable; Chapot/San Lucas; Steinkraus/Snowbound)
	Dublin	1st (Mary Chapot/White Lightning; Kusner/Fru; Chapot/San Lucas; Steinkraus/Snowbound)
	Ostend	1st (Mary Chapot/White Lightning; Kusner/Untouchable; Hofmann/ Out Late; Chapot/San Lucas)

APPENDIX—MAJOR USET VICTORIES

1968 Rotterdam — 1st (Mary Chapot/White Lightning; Hofmann/Out Late; Kusner/Untouchable; Chapot/San Lucas)

New York — 1st (Mary Chapot/White Lightning; Hofmann/Salem; Chapot/San Lucas; Steinkraus/Bold Minstrel)

Toronto — 1st (Shapiro/Trick Track; Mary Chapot/White Lightning; Chapot/San Lucas; Hofmann/Salem)

1969 Harrisburg — 1st (Shapiro/Trick Track; Brinsmade/Triple Crown; Chapot/San Lucas; Steinkraus/Bold Minstrel)

New York — 1st (Brinsmade/Triple Crown; Kusner/Wicked City; Chapot/San Lucas; Steinkraus/Bold Minstrel)

Toronto — 2nd to Canada

1970 Lucerne — 1st (Shapiro/San Lucas; Fargis/Bonte II; Kusner/Silver Scot; Steinkraus/Snowbound)

Aachen — 3rd to West Germany and Great Britain

La Baule — 3rd to Canada and France

Harrisburg — 2nd to West Germany

New York — 2nd to West Germany

Toronto — 2nd to West Germany

1971 Fontainebleau — 4th to West Germany, Italy and Great Britain

Aachen — 1st (Fargis/Bonte II; Homfeld/Triple Crown; Shapiro/Sloopy; Steinkraus/Fleet Apple)

Dublin — 4th to West Germany, Great Britain and Italy

Harrisburg — 1st (Fargis/Bonte II; Shapiro/Sloopy; Chapot/San Lucas; Steinkraus/Fleet Apple)

THE DE NÉMETHY YEARS

1971	New York	2nd to Canada
	Toronto	2nd to Canada
1972	Lucerne	3rd to West Germany and Switzerland
	Aachen	3rd to West Germany and Argentina
	Harrisburg	1st (Shapiro/Duke's Honor; Kusner/Triple Crown; Chapot/Good Twist; Steinkraus/Main Spring)
	New York	1st (Shapiro/Duke's Honor; Kusner/Triple Crown; Chapot/Good Twist; Steinkraus/Main Spring)
	Toronto	1st (Shapiro/Trick Track; Kusner/Triple Crown; Steinkraus/Main Spring; Chapot/Good Twist)
1973	Washington	1st (Jenkins/Idle Dice; Chapot/Main Spring; Matz/Snow Flurry; Cone/Triple Crown)
	New York	2nd to Great Britain
	London	1st (Cone/Triple Crown; Matz/Mighty Ruler; Jenkins/Idle Dice; Chapot/Main Spring)
1974	Lucerne	4th to Great Britain, West Germany and Switzerland
	La Baule	2nd to West Germany
	London	2nd to Great Britain
	Dublin	3rd to Great Britain and West Germany
	Washington	1st (Brown/Sandsablaze; Hardy/Comming Attraction; Murphy/Do Right; Jenkins/Number One Spy)
	New York	1st (Brown/Sandsablaze; Hardy/Coming Attraction; Murphy/Do Right; Chapot/Main Spring)
	Toronto	4th to France, Canada and Great Britain

APPENDIX—MAJOR USET VICTORIES

1975	Washington	1st (Shapiro/Jury Duster; Smith/Radnor II; Homfeld/Old English; Jenkins/Idle Dice)
	New York	1st (Brown/Sandsablaze; Matz/Grande; Murphy/Do Right; Jenkins/Idle Dice)
	Toronto	1st (Brown/Sandsablaze; Murphy/Do Right; Ridland/Southside; Jenkins/Idle Dice)
1976	Washington	1st (Frank Chapot/Coach Stop; Buddy Brown/Flying John; Michael Matz/Grande; Dennis Murphy/Do Right)
	New York	1st (Frank Chapot/Coach Stop; Buddy Brown/Flying John; Michael Matz/Grande; Dennis Murphy/Tuscaloosa)
	Toronto	1st (Frank Chapot/Coach Stop; Buddy Brown/Flying John; Michael Matz/Grande; Dennis Murphy/Tuscaloosa)
	Aachen	5th
	Lucerne	1st (Robert Ridland/Almost Persuaded; Dennis Murphy/Hummer; Michael Matz/Grande; Buddy Brown/Viscount)
1977	Washington	1st (Buddy Brown/Sandsablaze; Michael Matz/Jet Run; Conrad Homfeld/Balbuco; Joe Fargis/Pueblo)
	New York	1st (Buddy Brown/Sandsablaze; Michael Matz/Jet Run; Conrad Homfeld/Balbuco; Rodney Jenkins/Idle Dice)
	Toronto	2nd

1978	Washington	2nd to Canada
	New York	1st (Buddy Brown/Flying John; Dennis Murphy/Tuscaloosa; Melanie Smith/Val de Loire; Bernie Traurig/Gucci)
	Toronto	1st (Michael Matz/Sandor; Dennis Murphy/Tuscaloosa; Scott Nederlander/Southside; Robert Ridland/Nazarius)
	Calgary	3rd
	Aachen	8th
	Hickstead	2nd
	Rotterdam	1st (Conrad Homfeld/Balbuco; Michael Matz/Sandor; Dennis Murphy/Tuscaloosa; Robert Ridland/Nazarius)
1979	Washington	1st (Michael Matz/Jet Run; Melanie Smith/Calypso; Norman dello Joio/Allegro; Peter Leone/Semi Pro)
	New York	1st (Michael Matz/Jet Run; Melanie Smith/Val de Loire; Norman dello Joio/Allegro; Terry Rudd/Fat City)
	Toronto	2nd to Canada
	Calgary	2nd to Great Britain
1980	Washington	1st (Melanie Smith/Calypso; Leslie Burr/Chase the Clouds; Norman dello Joio/Allegro; Armand Leone, Semi Pro)
	New York	1st (Melanie Smith/Calypso; Leslie Burr/Chase the Clouds; Norman dello Joio/Allegro; Armand Leone, Jr./Wallenstein)

APPENDIX—MAJOR USET VICTORIES

1980 Toronto   2nd
         Calgary   5th
         Paris   3rd
         Dublin   1st (Melanie Smith/Calypso; Katie Monahan/Silver Exchange; Norman dello Joio/Allegro; Armand Leone, Jr./Wallenstein)
         Rotterdam   2nd to France

MAJOR EUROPEAN VICTORIES

1955	Le Zoute	Prix Savoy Hotel	William Steinkraus/ Night Owl
1956	London	King George V Gold Cup	William Steinkraus/ First Boy
		Country Life Cup	Frank Chapot/ Matador
	Dublin	Class No. 3	Frank Chapot/ Matador
		Class No. 5	Frank Chapot/ Defense
1958	Aachen	Preis Philips	William Steinkraus/ First Boy
		Preis Glas Industrie	George Morris/ War Bride
		German Federation Trophy	William Steinkraus/ First Boy
	London	Manifesto Stake	William Steinkraus/ Ksar d'Esprit
		Foxhunter Stakes	Hugh Wiley/ Nautical
		King George V Gold Cup	Hugh Wiley/Master William
	Dublin	Puissance	Hugh Wiley/ Nautical
		Américaine	George Morris/War Bride
		Ball's Bridge Stake	George Morris/ Sinjon
		Irish Trophy	George Morris/ Night Owl
		High Jump	Hugh Wiley/ Nautical

APPENDIX—MAJOR USET VICTORIES

1958	Ostend	Prix Pesage	George Morris/ Sinjon
		Prix Kursaal	William Steinkraus/ Ksar d'Esprit
		Grand Prix	William Steinkraus/ Ksar d'Esprit
		Prix Vainqueurs	Hugh Wiley/Master William
	Rotterdam	Puissance	William Steinkraus/ Ksar d'Esprit
		Grand Prix	William Steinkraus/ Ksar d'Esprit
1959	Wiesbaden	Puissance	William Steinkraus/ Ksar d'Esprit
	Paris	Prix Tuileries	Hugh Wiley/Master William
	Aachen	German Championship	William Steinkraus/ Riviera Wonder
	London	Manifesto Stake	Hugh Wiley/ Nautical
		Horse and Hound Cup	Hugh Wiley/ Nautical
		Nizefela Stake	William Steinkraus/ First Boy
		King George V Gold Cup	Hugh Wiley/ Nautical
		Daily Mail Cup	Hugh Wiley/ Nautical
1960	Wiesbaden	Grand Prix	William Steinkraus/ Riviera Wonder
	Lucerne	Preis Bürgenstock	George Morris/ Sinjon
		Preis Pilatus	George Morris/ Sinjon

161

THE DE NÉMETHY YEARS

1960		Preis Ermitage	William Steinkraus/ Riviera Wonder
		Preis Gütsch	George Morris/ High Noon
	Aachen	German Federation Trophy	George Morris/ High Noon
		Puissance	William Steinkraus/ Ksar d'Esprit
		Grand Prix	George Morris/ Night Owl
		3rd Qualification	William Steinkraus/ Riviera Wonder
	London	Horse and Hound Cup	George Morris/ Sinjon
		Tankard Stake	William Steinkraus/ Riviera Wonder
		Lonsdale Puissance	William Steinkraus/ Ksar d'Esprit
	Ostend	Prix Janssens	George Morris/ Sinjon
		Prix Kursaal	Hugh Wiley/Master William
		Grand Prix	William Steinkraus/ Ksar d'Esprit
	Venice	Puissance	William Steinkraus/ Ksar d'Esprit
1962	Aachen	Puissance	William Steinkraus/ Ksar d'Esprit
		Preis Philips	Frank Chapot/Night Owl
		1st Qualification	William Steinkraus/ Sinjon
		2nd Qualification	William Steinkraus/ Sinjon
	London	Country Life Cup	William Steinkraus/ Sinjon

APPENDIX—MAJOR USET VICTORIES

1962	Dublin	Pembroke Stake	William Steinkraus/Sinjon
		Puissance	Frank Chapot/San Lucas
1964	Hickstead	Emerald Stake	Kathy Kusner/Untouchable
	London	Imperial Cup	Mary Mairs/Anakonda
		King George V Gold Cup	William Steinkraus/Sinjon
		John Player Trophy	Mary Mairs/Tomboy
	Dublin	Pembroke Stake I	Frank Chapot/Manon
		Pembroke Stake II	Kathy Kusner/Untouchable
		Irish Trophy	Kathy Kusner/Untouchable
	Ostend	Prix Royal Palace	Kathy Kusner/Untouchable
		Prix Wellington	Carol Hofmann/Can't Tell
	Rotterdam	Pre-Olympic	Kathy Kusner/Untouchable
1966	Wiesbaden	Grand Prix	Frank Chapot/San Lucas
	Cologne	Grand Prix	Crystine Jones/Fru
	Lucerne	Preis Neu-Habsburg	Mary Chapot/White Lightning
		Preis-Seeburg	Kathy Kusner/Untouchable
		Grand Prix	Kathy Kusner/Untouchable
	Aachen	Preis Feuerversicherung	Frank Chapot/Good Twist
		Preis Landschaftsverband	Frank Chapot/Good Twist

1966		Puissance	Kathy Kusner/ Untouchable
		Américaine	Crystine Jones/Fru
		Röchling Preis	Frank Chapot/Good Twist and San Lucas
		Grand Prix	Neal Shapiro/Jacks or Better
	Essen	Grand Prix	Mary Chapot/ Tomboy
1967	Cologne	Grand Prix	William Steinkraus/ Bold Minstrel
	Aachen	Preis Olympische Gesellschaft	Frank Chapot/Good Twist
		Puissance	Kathy Kusner/ Aberali
	Hickstead	Class 34	Frank Chapot/Good Twist
		Class 41	Frank Chapot/Good Twist
1968	Hickstead	Ireland Stake	Kathy Kusner/ Untouchable
		Parcours de Chasse	Carol Hofmann/Out Late
	London	Nizefela Stakes	Kathy Kusner/Fru
		Queen Elizabeth Cup	Mary Chapot/White Lightning
		Daily Mail Cup	William Steinkraus/ Snowbound
		Last Chance	Neal Shapiro/Night Spree
	Dublin	Shellstar Stake	Carol Hofmann/Out Late
		BP Chase	Carol Hofmann/Out Late

APPENDIX—MAJOR USET VICTORIES

1968	Hickstead	Wills Stake	Kathy Kusner/Fru
	Ostend	Prix Henri Serruys	Carol Hofmann/Out Late
		Prix Wellington	Mary Chapot/White Lightning
		Prix du Champion	Frank Chapot/Good Twist
		Grand Prix	William Steinkraus/Blue Plum
		Puissance	William Steinkraus/Blue Plum
	Rotterdam	Jockey Club	Carol Hofmann/Out Late
		Américaine	Kathy Kusner/Fru
		Grand Prix	Carol Hofmann/Out Late
1970	Lucerne	Preis Bürgenstock	William Steinkraus/Snowbound
		Preis Seeburg	William Steinkraus/Bold Minstrel
		Preis Kanton Luzern	William Steinkraus/Snowbound
		Preis St. Georg	William Steinkraus/Bold Minstrel
		Preis St. Gotthard	Robert Ridland/Blue Plum; Kathy Kusner/Night Hawk
		Preis Gütsch	William Steinkraus/Bold Minstrel
	Wülfrath	Grand Prix	Kathy Kusner/Silver Scot
	Aachen	Hilko Preis	William Steinkraus/Snowbound
		Américaine Preis	Kathy Kusner/Fru William Steinkraus/

THE DE NÉMETHY YEARS

1970		Actien-brauerei Orlik Preis	Snowbound
			Frank Chapot/White Lightning
	La Baule	Class No. 3	Frank Chapot/San Lucas
		Class No. 6	Frank Chapot/San Lucas
		Relay	Robert Ridland/Blue Plum; Kathy Kusner/Fru
1971	Aachen	Preis Kreiss-parkasse	Robert Ridland/ Charles Stewart
		Hilko Preis	William Steinkraus/ Fleet Apple
		Röchling Preis	William Steinkraus/ Snowbound and Fleet Apple
		Grand Prix	Neal Shapiro/Sloopy
	Hickstead	Three Castle Stakes	William Steinkraus/ Fleet Apple
	London	Horse and Hound Cup	Neal Shapiro/Sloopy
		John Player Trophy	William Steinkraus/ Fleet Apple
1972	Wiesbaden	Grand Prix	Kathy Kusner/ Triple Crown
	Lucerne	Gübelin Preis	William Steinkraus/ Main Spring
		Heliomalt Preis	Kathy Kusner/ Nirvana
	Aachen	Münchner Versicherung	William Steinkraus/ Main Spring
		Rheinland Preis	Robert Ridland/ Almost Persuaded

APPENDIX—MAJOR USET VICTORIES

1972		Juvena Preis	Frank Chapot/White Lightning
		Zentis Preis	Kathy Kusner/ Nirvana
	La Baule	Criterium Champions	Kathy Kusner/ Triple Crown
		Class No. 3	Neal Shapiro/Duke's Honor
1974	Lucerne	Relay	Buddy Brown/A Little Bit; Robert Ridland/Flying John
		Grand Prix	Robert Ridland/ Almost Persuaded
	La Baule	2nd Qualification	Michele McEvoy/ Mr. Muskie
	Hickstead	Chasse	Dennis Murphy/Do Right
		Speed Stake	Dennis Murphy/ Tuscaloosa
	London	King George V Gold Cup	Frank Chapot/Main Spring
		John Player Trophy	Rodney Jenkins/ Number One Spy
		Calor Glass	Buddy Brown/A Little Bit
		Puissance	Robert Ridland/ Almost Persuaded
	Cardiff	1st Leg Championship	Rodney Jenkins/ Number One Spy
		Match Play	Rodney Jenkins/ Idle Dice
	Dublin	BP Chase	Buddy Brown/ Sandsablaze
		Top Score	Dennis Murphy/ Tuscaloosa

THE DE NÉMETHY YEARS

1974		Six Bars	Rodney Jenkins/ Idle Dice
		Irish Trophy	Buddy Brown/ Sandsablaze
1976	Wiesbaden	Grand Prix	Buddy Brown/A Little Bit
	Cologne	Class S	Kathy Kusner/ Singapore
1978	Wülfrath	Class M	Buddy Brown/ Garham Girl
		Qualifier for Grand Prix	Dennis Murphy/Do Right
	Aachen	Preis des Aachener Steinkohlen- berghaus	Dennis Murphy/ Tuscaloosa
		Qualifier for Championship	Michael Matz/ Sandor
		Philips	Buddy Brown/Idle Dice
		Dresdner Bank	Buddy Brown/ Garham Girl
	Wolfsburg	Class M	Dennis Murphy/ Commodore
		Kurzparcours	Dennis Murphy/ Tuscaloosa
		Schenker	Dennis Murphy/ Tuscaloosa
	Arena North	Lakeside	Dennis Murphy/Do Right
		Cabaret	Dennis Murphy/ Tuscaloosa
		Mappin Plate	Michael Matz/Jet Run
		International Velvet	Buddy Brown/ Viscount

APPENDIX—MAJOR USET VICTORIES

1978	Hickstead	Castella Cigar	Dennis Murphy/ Commodore
		Lambert & Butler Pair Relay	Buddy Brown/ Garham Girl & Michael Matz/ Grande
	Aachen World Championship	Class 1B	Dennis Murphy/Do Right
		Class 4	Michael Matz/Jet Run
	Rotterdam	Top Score	Conrad Homfeld/ Pueblo
1980	Paris	Grand Prix	Melanie Smith/ Calypso
	Hickstead	Castella Cigar	Norman Dello Joio/ Johnny's Pocket
		Lambert & Butler	Melanie Smith/ Vivaldi
		Fault & Out	Katie Monahan/ Silver Exchange
	Wembley	Grand Prix	Terry Rudd/Semi Tough
		Philips Trial	Norman Dello Joio/ Johnny's Pocket
		Horse & Hound	Melanie Smith/ Calypso
		Puissance	Armand Leone, Jr./ Wallenstein
	Dublin	MSD Stakes	Melanie Smith/ Calypso
		Accumulator	Dennis Murphy/ Lyrical Lou
	Rotterdam	Prix du Cercle Equestre	Armand Leone, Jr./ Encore
		Prix de van Nelle	Melanie Smith/ Calypso

169

NORTH AMERICAN FALL CIRCUIT VICTORIES

1955	Harrisburg	Penn State Police	Charles Dennehy/ Altmeister
		Low Score 2, 3	Dennehy, Wiley, Steinkraus
	New York	President of Mexico Trophy	William Steinkraus/ Saxon Wood and Can Can
		West Point Trophy	William Steinkraus/ Saxon Wood
		Stake	William Steinkraus/ Saxon Wood
		Winter Fair Trophy	Charles Dennehy/ Altmeister
	Toronto	Low Score 2, 3	Dennehy, Wiley, Steinkraus
		Fault and Out	Charles Dennehy/ Pill Box
1956	Harrisburg	Henry Trophy	Frank Chapot/ Matador
		Low Score 2, 3	Chapot, Steinkraus, Wiley
	New York	Drake Memorial	Hugh Wiley/ Nautical
		Stone Trophy	Frank Chapot/ Defense
	Toronto	Class A	William Steinkraus/ First Boy
1956	Toronto	Puissance	Hugh Wiley/ Nautical
		Team Class A	Chapot, Steinkraus, Wiley
		Two and Two	Chapot, Steinkraus, Wiley

APPENDIX—MAJOR USET VICTORIES

1957	Harrisburg	Henry Trophy	Frank Chapot/ Moonflight
		Low Score 3	Wiley, Steinkraus, Chapot
	New York	West Point Trophy	Hugh Wiley/ Nautical
		Stone Trophy	Hugh Wiley/ Nautical
		Stake	Hugh Wiley/ Nautical
		Low Score 2, 3	Wiley, Steinkraus, Chapot
	Toronto	Individual	Frank Chapot/ Pill Box
		Fault and Out	Hugh Wiley/ Nautical
		Puissance	Hugh Wiley/ Nautical
1958	Washington	Stake	Frank Chapot/ Trail Guide
1958	Harrisburg	Penn Stake Police Stake	Hugh Wiley/ Nautical William Steinkraus/ Ksar d'Esprit
		Low Score 2	Chapot, Steinkraus, Wiley
	New York	West Point Trophy	Hugh Wiley/ Nautical
		President of Mexico Trophy	William Steinkraus/ Diamant and Ksar d'Esprit
		Low Score 1	Chapot, Steinkraus, Wiley
		Good Will Trophy	William Steinkraus/ Ksar d'Esprit
		Stone Trophy	Hugh Wiley/ Nautical

THE DE NÉMETHY YEARS

1958	Toronto	Fault and Out	Frank Chapot/ Trail Guide
		Jumping Table C	Hugh Wiley/ Nautical
		Championship	William Steinkraus/ Ksar d'Esprit
1959	Harrisburg	Championship	William Steinkraus/ Trail Guide
		Stake	Frank Chapot/ Springboard
		International Team	Chapot, Steinkraus, Wiley
1959	Washington	Two Horse	William Steinkraus/ Ksar d'Esprit and Trail Guide
		Preliminary	Frank Chapot/ Tally Ho
		Speed	Hugh Wiley/ Nautical
		Table A	Hugh Wiley/ Nautical
		Speed	Hugh Wiley/ Nautical
		Table A	Hugh Wiley/ Master William
	New York	Democrat Trophy	William Steinkraus/ Trail Guide
		Drake Memorial	William Steinkraus/ Riviera Wonder
		Puissance	William Steinkraus/ Ksar d'Esprit
		Stake	Hugh Wiley/ Nautical
		Low Score 2	Steinkraus, Wiley, Chapot

APPENDIX—MAJOR USET VICTORIES

1959		Championship	William Steinkraus/ Riviera Wonder
		Two and Two	Chapot, Steinkraus, Morris
	Toronto	Fault and Out	George Morris/ Sinjon
		Championship	William Steinkraus/ Trail Guide
		Stake	William Steinkraus/ Trail Guide
1960	Harrisburg	Penn Lodge Trophy	Frank Chapot/ Tally Ho
		Low Score 1, 2, 3	Chapot, Wiley, Morris
		Championship	Frank Chapot/ Tally Ho
		Stake	Frank Chapot/ Trail Guide
	Washington	Abendroth Trophy	Frank Chapot/ Diamant
		Humphrey Trophy	George Morris/ Sinjon
		Martin Trophy	George Morris/ High Noon
		Puissance	Hugh Wiley/ Ksar d'Esprit
	New York	West Point Trophy	Frank Chapot/ Trail Guide
		Good Will Trophy	George Morris/ High Noon
		Stake	Hugh Wiley/ Nautical
		Low Score 1, 2, 3	Chapot, Morris, Wiley
	Toronto	Puissance	Hugh Wiley/ Ksar d'Esprit

THE DE NÉMETHY YEARS

1960		Jumping Table C	George Morris/ Sinjon
		Team Class A	Chapot, Morris, Wiley
		Two and Two	Chapot, Morris, Wiley
1961	Harrisburg	28th Infantry Trophy	William Steinkraus/ Ksar d'Esprit
		Fault and Out	Frank Chapot/ Diamant
		Puissance	William Steinkraus/ Ksar d'Esprit
		Penn Lodge Trophy	William Steinkraus/ Lilly Buck
		Stake	Frank Chapot/ Night Owl
		Gamblers Choice	William Steinkraus/ Ksar d'Esprit
		Championship	William Steinkraus/ Ksar d'Esprit
	Washington	President's Cup Qualification	Frank Chapot/ San Lucas
	New York	Fault and Out	Kathy Kusner/ High Noon
		Championship	Frank Chapot/ San Lucas
	Toronto	Puissance	William Steinkraus/ Ksar d'Esprit
		McKee Stake	Frank Chapot/ San Lucas
		Team Class A	Chapot, Steinkraus, Kusner
1962	Harrisburg	28th Infantry Trophy	William Steinkraus/ Sinjon

APPENDIX—MAJOR USET VICTORIES

1962		Fault and Out	Frank Chapot/ Shady Lady
		Puissance	William Steinkraus/ Fire One
		Scurry	Frank Chapot/ Shady Lady
		Gamblers Choice	Frank Chapot/ San Lucas
		Stake	William Steinkraus/ Fire One
	Washington	Chechi Trophy	Mary Mairs/Tomboy
		Martins Trophy	Carol Hofmann/ Le Bon Chat
		President's Cup	Kathy Kusner/ Unusual
	New York	McKay Trophy	Frank Chapot/ San Lucas
		Democrat Trophy	William Steinkraus/ Sinjon
		Murray Memorial	Steinkraus, Mairs, Chapot
		Good Will Trophy	William Steinkraus/ Fire One
	Toronto	Welcome Stake	Frank Chapot/ San Lucas
		Puissance	Frank Chapot/ San Lucas

1963	Harrisburg	Preliminary	Frank Chapot/ Shady Lady
		Fault and Out	William Steinkraus/ Sinjon
		Puissance	Frank Chapot/ Manon
		Championship	Frank Chapot/ Manon

175

1963		White Trophy	Frank Chapot/ Shady Lady
		Stake	William Steinkraus/ Sinjon
		Qualifying	tied { William Steinkraus/ Fire One, Kathy Kusner/ Untouchable }
	Washington	Ecuador Trophy	Frank Chapot/ Manon
		Puissance	Frank Chapot/ San Lucas
		Martins Trophy	Frank Chapot/ Shady Lady
		Washington Stake	Mary Mairs/Tomboy
	New York	Good Will Trophy	Frank Chapot/ Manon
		Stake	William Steinkraus/ Sinjon
	Toronto	Team Class A	Chapot, Mairs, Kusner
		Welcome Stake	William Steinkraus/ Sinjon
		Puissance	Frank Chapot/ San Lucas
1964	Harrisburg	Puissance	Neal Shapiro/Jacks or Better
		Fault and Out	Neal Shapiro/Jacks or Better
		Preliminary	James Saurino/ Blenheim's Buck
		Speed Class	Carol Hofmann/ Can't Tell
		Gamblers Choice	Neal Shapiro/Jacks or Better

APPENDIX—MAJOR USET VICTORIES

1964		Two Horse Class	Bill Robertson/ Norwich and The Sheriff
	New York	Democrat Trophy	Kathy Kusner/ Untouchable
		Mackay Trophy	Kathy Kusner/ Untouchable
		Pennsylvania Trophy	Frank Chapot/ Shady Lady
		Puissance	William Steinkraus/ San Lucas
		Good Will Trophy	Frank Chapot/ Manon
		Grand Prix of North America	Kathy Kusner/ Untouchable
		Murray Trophy	Chapot, Kusner, Shapiro
	Toronto	Welcome Stake	Kathy Kusner/ Untouchable
		Puissance	tied { Kathy Kusner/ Untouchable, Frank Chapot/ Manon }
		Maple Leaf	William Steinkraus/ Sinjon
		Rothman Stake	William Steinkraus/ Sinjon
		McKee Stake	Kathy Kusner/ Untouchable
		Team Class A	Chapot, Kusner, Steinkraus
1965	Harrisburg	Preliminary	Kathy Kusner/ Untouchable
		Table A	Frank Chapot/ Anakonda

1965		Fault and Out	Kathy Kusner/That's Right
		Jump-Off	Mary Chapot/Tomboy
		Take Own Line	William Steinkraus/Snowbound
	New York	Table A	Mary Chapot/Manon
		Team Speed	Chapot, Kusner, Steinkraus
		West Point Trophy	Frank Chapot/Manon
		Americana Trophy	William Steinkraus/Sinjon
		MacKay Trophy	Kathy Kusner/Unusual
		Puissance	Frank Chapot/San Lucas
		Good Will Trophy	Mary Chapot/Anakonda
		Stake	Mary Chapot/Tomboy
		Black and White Trophy	Kathy Kusner/Unusual
		Grand Prix	William Steinkraus/Snowbound
	Washington	Ringmaster Trophy	Kathy Kusner/Fire One
		Martins Trophy	Mary Chapot/White Lightning
		Ecuador Trophy	Kathy Kusner/Unusual
		Puissance	Frank Chapot/San Lucas
		President's Cup Preliminary	Kathy Kusner/Unusual
		President's Cup	Frank Chapot/San Lucas

APPENDIX—MAJOR USET VICTORIES

1965		Stake	Frank Chapot/ San Lucas
	Toronto	Team Class A	Chapot, Chapot, Kusner
		Gamblers Stake	Mary Chapot/ Tomboy
		Doubles and Trebles	Frank Chapot/ Good Twist
		Welcome Stakes	Mary Chapot/ Tomboy
		One Chance	Carol Hofmann/ Can't Tell
		Puissance	Frank Chapot/ San Lucas
		North American Championship	Frank Chapot/ San Lucas
1966	Harrisburg	Time Class	Mary Chapot/ Anakonda
		Puissance	Frank Chapot/ San Lucas
		Stake	Mary Chapot/ Tomboy
		International Individual	William Steinkraus/ Snowbound
	New York	West Point Trophy	Kathy Kusner/ Aberali
		Democrat Trophy	William Steinkraus/ Snowbound
		Good Will Trophy	Kathy Kusner/ Untouchable
		Black and White Trophy	Kathy Kusner/ Untouchable
		Pennsylvania Trophy	Mary Chapot/White Lightning
		Royal Winter Fair	Frank Chapot/ Good Twist

179

THE DE NÉMETHY YEARS

1966		Grand Prix	Mary Chapot/ Tomboy
	Washington	Martins Trophy	Carol Hofmann/ Salem
		Puissance	Kathy Kusner/ Untouchable
		President's Cup Preliminary	Frank Chapot/ Good Twist
		President's Cup	Crystine Jones/ Trick Track
		Stake	Kathy Kusner/ Untouchable
	Toronto	One Chance	Frank Chapot/ Good Twist
		Puissance	Frank Chapot/ San Lucas
		Doubles and Trebles	Frank Chapot/ Good Twist
1967	Harrisburg	28th Infantry Trophy	William Steinkraus/ Bold Minstrel
		Puissance	William Steinkraus/ Bold Minstrel
		Doubles and Trebles	Crystine Jones/ Ksarina
		Tandems	William Steinkraus/ Bold Minstrel and Snowbound
		Grand Prix	Mary Chapot/ Anakonda
	Washington	President's Cup	Neal Shapiro/ Night Spree
	New York	West Point Trophy	Mary Chapot/ Manon
		Democrat Trophy	Neal Shapiro/ Night Spree
		Puissance	William Steinkraus/ Bold Minstrel

APPENDIX—MAJOR USET VICTORIES

1967		Good Will Trophy	Carol Hofmann/ Salem
		Black and White	Mary Chapot/ Anakonda
		Pennsylvania Trophy	Kathy Kusner/ Aberali
		Royal Winter Fair	Carol Hofmann/ Salem
	Toronto	Welcome Stake	Kathy Kusner/ Aberali
		International Stake	Mary Chapot/ Anakonda
		Scurry Stake	Mary Chapot/Manon
		Gamblers Stake	Neal Shapiro/Night Spree
		Doubles and Trebles	Kathy Kusner/ Untouchable
		Championship	Kathy Kusner/ Untouchable
1968	Harrisburg	28th Infantry Trophy	Jared Brinsmade/ Triple Crown
		Puissance	Joan Boyce/In My Cup
		Doubles and Trebles Stake	Jared Brinsmade/ Triple Crown
		Gay Wiles/Manon	
	Washington	President's Cup	Jared Brinsmade/ Triple Crown
		Ringmaster Trophy	Gay Wiles/The Senator
		Puissance	Neal Shapiro/Trick Track
		Table A	Neal Shapiro/Trick Track
		Jump-Off	Jared Brinsmade/ Triple Crown

181

1968	New York	MacKay Trophy Stake	Kathy Kusner/Fru Carol Hofmann/ Salem
		Grand Prix	Mary Chapot/White Lightning
	Toronto	Bate Trophy	Carol Hofmann/ Out Late
		Puissance	Frank Chapot/ San Lucas
		Doubles and Trebles	Mary Chapot/White Lightning
		Speed Stake	Carol Hofmann/ Out Late
		McKee Stake	Frank Chapot/ San Lucas
1969	Harrisburg	National Horse Show Trophy	William Steinkraus/ Bold Minstrel
		28th Infantry Trophy	Neal Shapiro/Manon
		Fault and Out	Frank Chapot/White Lightning
		Grand Prix	Jared Brinsmade/ Triple Crown
	Washington	Eisenhower Trophy	Jared Brinsmade/ Golden Gavel
		Ringmaster Trophy	Jared Brinsmade/ Golden Gavel
		President's Cup Preliminary	Frank Chapot/White Lightning
	New York	West Point Trophy	Frank Chapot/White Lightning
		Democrat Trophy	William Steinkraus/ Bold Minstrel
		MacKay Trophy	Frank Chapot/White Lightning
		National Horse Show Cup	Kathy Kusner/ That's Right

APPENDIX—MAJOR USET VICTORIES

1969		Stake	William Steinkraus/ Bold Minstrel
		Royal Winter Fair	William Steinkraus/ Bold Minstrel
	Toronto	International Stake	Frank Chapot/ San Lucas
		Scurry	Frank Chapot/White Lightning
		Doubles and Trebles	Kathy Kusner/ That's Right
		Speed Stake	Jared Brinsmade/ Rome Dome
1970	Washington	Opening Class	Conrad Homfeld/ Bonte II
		Eisenhower Trophy	Carol Hofmann/ Salem
	New York	Democrat Trophy	William Steinkraus/ Bold Minstrel
		Puissance	Frank Chapot/ San Lucas
		Good Will Trophy	Frank Chapot/White Lightning
1971	Harrisburg	Opening Class	Joe Fargis/Bonte II
		Puissance	Frank Chapot/ San Lucas
		Police Trophy	Joe Fargis/Bonte II
		Grand Prix	Neal Shapiro/Sloopy
	Washington	President's Cup Preliminary	Joe Fargis/Bonte II
	New York	Democrat Trophy	William Steinkraus/ Fleet Apple
		MacKay Trophy	Carol Hofmann/ Salem
		Volco Trophy	Frank Chapot/White Lightning

1971		Good Will Trophy	Neal Shapiro/ Nirvana
		Stake	Joe Fargis/Bonte II
		Grand Prix	Robert Ridland/ Almost Persuaded
	Toronto	Rothman Stake	Carol Hofmann/ Salem
		Relay	Frank Chapot, Carol Hofmann
		Américaine	Joe Fargis/San Lucas
		Championship	Joe Fargis/San Lucas
		McKee Stake	Frank Chapot/ Good Twist
		Fault and Out	Frank Chapot/ Good Twist
1972	Harrisburg	Preliminary	Frank Chapot/ Good Twist
		International Individual	William Steinkraus/ Main Spring
		Puissance	Kathy Kusner/ Nirvana
		International Individual	Kathy Kusner/ Nirvana
		International Individual	William Steinkraus/ Main Spring
		International Individual	William Steinkraus/ Main Spring
		Grand Prix	Frank Chapot/ Good Twist
	Washington	Fault and Out	Kathy Kusner/ Nirvana
	New York	Cavcote Trophy	Kathy Kusner/ Nirvana
		Democrat Trophy	Frank Chapot/ Good Twist

APPENDIX—MAJOR USET VICTORIES

1972		MacKay Trophy	Frank Chapot/ Good Twist
		Puissance	Neal Shapiro/Trick Track
		Volco Trophy	William Steinkraus/ Main Spring
		Table A	Kathy Kusner/ Nirvana
		Stake	William Steinkraus/ Main Spring
		Fault and Out	Frank Chapot/White Lightning
		Table A	Frank Chapot/ Good Twist
		Grand Prix	Frank Chapot/ Good Twist
	Toronto	Class	Neal Shapiro/Trick Track
		Fault and Out	Mac Cone/Bomber
		Championship	William Steinkraus/ Main Spring
1973	Washington	Welcome Stake	Rodney Jenkins/ Balbuco
		Bonus Class	Frank Chapot/ Main Spring
		Puissance	Rodney Jenkins/ Idle Dice
	New York	MacKay Trophy	Frank Chapot/ Good Twist
		Volco Trophy	Frank Chapot/ Main Spring
		National Horse Show Cup	Rodney Jenkins/ Idle Dice
		Grand Prix	Rodney Jenkins/ Idle Dice
	Toronto	Rothman Stake	Frank Chapot/ Good Twist

THE DE NÉMETHY YEARS

1973		Scurry	Rodney Jenkins/ Idle Dice
		Fault and Out	Rodney Jenkins/ Idle Dice
		Puissance	Rodney Jenkins/ Idle Dice
		Championship	Frank Chapot/ Main Spring
1974	Washington	Inverness Trophy	Rodney Jenkins/ Number One Spy
		Accumulator	Dennis Murphy/ Tuscaloosa
		Speed Class	Rodney Jenkins/ Idle Dice
		Martin Trophy	Rodney Jenkins/ Idle Dice
	New York	Democrat Trophy	Buddy Brown/ Sandsablaze
		Puissance	Dennis Murphy/ Do Right
	Toronto	Doubles and Trebles	Rodney Jenkins/ Number One Spy
		Hit and Hurry	Rodney Jenkins/ Idle Dice
		Fault and Out	Dennis Murphy/ Tuscaloosa
		Puissance	Dennis Murphy/ Do Right
		Championship	Frank Chapot/ Main Spring
		Fuller Speed	Dennis Murphy/ Tuscaloosa
1975	Washington	Speed Class	Rodney Jenkins/ Idle Dice
		Accumulator	Rodney Jenkins/ Idle Dice

APPENDIX—MAJOR USET VICTORIES

1975 President's Cup Rodney Jenkins/
                     Preliminary   Number One Spy
                     Speed Class   Rodney Jenkins/
                                           Idle Dice

     New York   Democrat   Dennis Murphy/
                     Trophy   Do Right
                   MacKay Trophy Rodney Jenkins/
                                           Idle Dice
                   Volco Trophy   Rodney Jenkins/
                                           Number One Spy
                   Classic   Rodney Jenkins/
                       Magazine   Idle Dice
                   Stake   Rodney Jenkins/
                                         Number One Spy
                   Grand Prix   Rodney Jenkins/
                                         Number One Spy

     Toronto   Welcome Stake Rodney Jenkins/
                                         Number One Spy
                   Rothman Stake Rodney Jenkins/
                                         Idle Dice
                   Open Stake   Dennis Murphy/
                                         Do Right
                   Fault and Out   Rodney Jenkins/
                                         Idle Dice
                   Puissance   Robert Ridland/
                                         Almost Persuaded
                                           Buddy Brown/
                                         Sandsablaze
                   Jigsaw   Robert Ridland,
                                         Buddy Brown
                   Championship   Robert Ridland/
                                         South Side

1976   Washington Accumulator   Dennis Murphy/
                                                    Tuscaloosa
     New York   Democrat   Michael Matz/
                                                    Grande

THE DE NÉMETHY YEARS

1976	Toronto	Fuller Speed	Michael Matz/ Grande
		Hit & Hurray	Dennis Murphy/ Tuscaloosa
1977	Washington	Faults Converted	Buddy Brown/ Sandsablaze
		Doubles & Trebles	Buddy Brown/ Sandsablaze
		Grand Prix	Buddy Brown/ Sandsablaze
	New York	Stone	Buddy Brown/ Sandsablaze
		Gucci	Buddy Brown/ Sandsablaze
	Toronto	Welcome	Bernie Traurig/ Fair Warning
		Fault & Out	Bernie Traurig/ Fair Warning
		Doubles & Trebles	Michael Matz/Jet Run
		Rothmans Stake	Buddy Brown/ Sandsablaze
		Scurry	Buddy Brown/ Viscount
		Grand Prix	Michael Matz/Jet Run
1978	Washington	Ringmaster	Dennis Murphy/ Tuscaloosa
		Inverness	Bernie Traurig/ The Cardinal
		Accumulator	Buddy Brown/ Idle Dice
		Eisenhower	Dennis Murphy/ Tuscaloosa
		Speed Stake	Dennis Murphy/ Do Right

APPENDIX—MAJOR USET VICTORIES

1978	New York	Stone	Melanie Smith/ Val de Loire
		Cole	Melanie Smith/ Radnor II
	Toronto	Hit & Hurry	Dennis Murphy/ Do Right
		Doubles & Trebles	Dennis Murphy/ Tuscaloosa
		Fuller Speed	Dennis Murphy/ Do Right
		Imperial Bank	Robert Ridland/ Nazarius
		Puissance	Robert Ridland/ Almost Persuaded
1979	New York	Cavcote	Melanie Smith/ Calypso
		Stone	Michael Matz/Jet Run
		Gucci	Michael Matz/Jet Run
		Grand Prix	Michael Matz/Jet Run
	Toronto	Hit & Hurry	Norman dello Joio/ Johnny's Pocket
		Doubles & Trebles	Melanie Smith/ Val de Loire
1980	Washington	Ringmaster	Leslie Burr/Friar Tuck
		Inverness	Leslie Burr/Chase the Clouds
	New York	Gucci	Melanie Smith/ Val de Loire
	Toronto	Welcome	Norman dello Joio/ Johnny's Pocket
		Scurry	Norman dello Joio/ Johnny's Pocket

189

1980 Johnston Michael Matz/Jet Run
  Power & Speed Michael Matz/Honest Tom
  Fuller Speed Melanie Smith/Vivaldi
  McKee Michael Matz/Jet Run

Index

A

Aachen International Stake, 70
Aids, application of, 8
Amateur Owner course, 103
Ambassador, 89
American Horse Shows Association (AHSA), 42, 66, 104, 105, 136
Americans, in competitions abroad, 40, 42, 43, 46–53, 58, 118–119. *See also* Olympic Games, Pan American Games, and United States Equestrian Team.
Amman, Max, 94
Anakonda, 65
Anatomy, horse's, 12
Andante, 67
Anderson, Gunnar, 68
Arambide, Hugo, 93
Arbitrage, 136
Arete, 90

B

Balance, 7, 8, 16
 forward, 15
Bambi, 90
Banbury, Clint, 92
Beethoven II, 136
Belair, 81
"Bert: The de Némethy Touch in American Riding," 114
Bizard, Captain Xavier, 33
Boulder Brook Club, 44, 67
Brady, James Cox, 44
Brinckmann, Hans Heinrich, 33
British Show Jumping Association, 40
Broome, David, 69, 86
Brown, Buddy, 72, 89, 92, 93
Bunn, Douglas, 126
Butler, Patrick, 58

C

Caesar, 92
Calypso, 106, 107, 138

INDEX

Caprilli, Federico, 10, 11
Cavalletti, 6, 7, 11, 12, 16, 24, 48, 68, 97, 116–118, 119, 133
Chamberlin, Harry D., 14
Championship of Brussels, 65
Chapot, Frank, 3, 59, 61, 62, 64, 65, 67–73, 81, 82, 84, 89, 91, 92, 136, 139
Cheeca Farm, 65
CHIO, 80
The Chronicle of the Horse, 94
Cin-a-Bit, 67
Clinics, de Némethy, 5–11, 13, 14
  courses, 24, 25
Club Hípico Costa Azúl de Alamar, 75
Coakes, Marion, 86
Collection, 14–15
Concours Saute International (CSI), 57, 58
Concours Saute International Officiel (CSIO), 58
Confidence, building rider's, 10
Coup Vetivier, 69
Course design, 40
  Atlantic City International Equestrian Festival, 106
  de Némethy on, 97–107
  Olympic, 101, 119
  World Cup, 100–103
Courses, clinic, 24, 25
"Crest release," 10
Cristi, Oscar, 90
Currier, S.R., 67

D

Daily Mail cup, 63
Delia, Carlos, 90, 91
d'Endrody, Captain A., 31
de La Valette, Luis, 75, 76
de Leon, Raul, 11, 12
de Leyer, Harry, 67, 68
dello Joio, Norman, 72, 93
de Némethy, Bertalan, 3, 5, 14, 17, 19, 21, 46, 113–115, 119–121, 129, 130, 132
  and junior competitors, 133–134, 136
  and the future, 136–142
  and the Olympics, 80–90
  and the Pan American Games, 90–94
  as coach of the USET, 47–53, 57, 58, 59–76, 80–94, 97, 138
  clinics, 5–11, 13, 14, 24, 25
  early experience with thoroughbreds, 31
  early years, 29–36
  influence of, 121, 126
  method, 15–16
  on cavalletti work, 116–118
  on course design, 97–107
  one rider's view of, 12–14
  on equitation, 104
  on lungeing, 115–116
  on importance of international exposure, 118–119
  on Olympic jumping, 23
  on show jumping, 22
  School of Riding, 24
  views on riding, 6, 7, 100
Dennehy, Charles, 91
Devereaux, Mrs. Walter B., 67
Diamant, 67
d'Inzeo, Raimondo, 82
Disney, Walt, 60
d'Oriola, Pierre, 22
Downton, Kyra, 92
Draw reins, 17
Dressage, 49, 114, 119, 130, 132
  classic, 12, 13, 14
  elementary, 9
  Haute Ecole, 16
  Third Level, 114
Dudley Do Right, 92
Durand, Carol, 46

E

Echevarría, Ricardo, 90
"Engagement," 15
Equestrian Ambassadors, 53
Equestrian sports, interest in, 130, 132
Equitation, 133
  de Némethy on, 104

INDEX

F

Fairfield Club, 44
Fargis, Joe, 72, 92
Fédération Equestre International (FEI), 5, 42, 46, 58, 72, 101, 136
Fire II, 106, 107
First Boy, 67
Fleet Apple, 89
Foltenyi, Gabor, 36, 46, 75
Forward-riding style, 10, 11, 14
Fritz, John H. (Jack), 45, 50

G

Gabathuler, Walter, 136
Galvin, Patricia (Mrs. John), 64–65, 67, 91
Gayford, Tom, 71
German Challenge Trophy, 66
Gladstone, 44, 45, 52, 70, 98, 118, 139
"Gladstone" style of riding, 48
Gold Lodge, 67
Good Twist, 65
Goyoaga, Paco, 61
Grande, 92
Grand Prix, 3, 5, 10, 15, 65, 68, 69, 71, 75, 104, 133, 139
Gunther, Bubbi, 33
Gunther, Maria, 8

H

Haggard, William D., 65
Hamburg Derby, 46, 70
Hamilton Farm, 44, 45
Hanover Cavalry School, 11
Hanson, Christilot, 92
Haskell, Amory, 43
Hasse, Ernst, 33
Hasse, Kurt, 33
Haute Ecole dressage, 16
Helsinki Olympics, 63, 67
Henry, General Guy V., 48
Heuckeroth, Otto, 68
High Jump Over Poles, 63
High Noon, 67, 69
Homfeld, Conrad, 133
Homm, Colonel Hally, 33

Honest Tom, 106, 107
Horse and Hound cup, 63, 68
Horse Play, 114, 132
Horses
  anatomy of, 12
  and jumping, 39–40
  cavalry's need for, 39
  flying abroad, 58
The Horse With the Flying Tail, 60
Hunter courses, 104–105
Hunters, 104–105, 113, 114

I

Individual Championship Challenge Trophy, 66
Intermediate course, 103
International competition, importance of for Americans, 118–119
International Equestrian Competition Corporation (IECC), 43
International Equestrian Festival, Atlantic City, 106
International Team Jumping Championship, 72

J

Jacks or Better, 71
Jenkins, Rodney, 44, 136
Jones, Chrystine, 3, 73, 75, 139
Junior competitors, 133–136, 139
Junior Olympics, 70
Jumpers, 113, 114
Jumping, 6, 7, 11, 13, 14, 16, 17, 19, 22, 40, 113–115
  cavalletti work, 6, 7, 11, 12, 16, 24, 48, 68, 97, 116–118, 199, 133
  course design for, 40, 97–107
  show, 37–43, 46–53, 136
"Jumping pirouette," 114

K

Kadett, 92
King George V Cup, 57, 61, 63
Koof, Norbert, 106, 107

193

INDEX

Ksar d'Esprit, 59, 63, 67, 69, 82
Kusner, Kathy, 19, 48, 59, 71, 72, 89, 92

L

Lafrenz, Marie C., 67, 70
Larraguibel, Alberto, 90
Larrain, Joaquin, 90
Le Dauphin, 92
Lequio, Colonel Tommaso, 33
Lewis, John, 33
Littauer, Vladimir S., 14, 15, 133
Lörke, Otto, 33
Ludovica Academy, 30
Lungeing, 8, 17, 115–116, 119, 139

M

McCashin, Arthur, 34, 46, 63, 67, 80, 91
Mclain Street, 70
Maclay finals, 104
Mahler, Mrs. Ernest, 67
Mainspring, 65, 87
Mairs, Mary, 19, 48, 59, 64, 70–71, 84, 91, 92
Mancinelli, Graziano, 89
Manon, 65, 71
Mariles, Humberto, 90, 93
Master William, 59, 63, 67, 82
Matz, Michael, 72, 89, 92, 93, 106, 107, 139
Medal finals, 104, 120
Mexico Olympics, 65, 84–86, 116, 118
Military Team Competition Division, 42
Millar, Torchy, 92
Monahan, Katie, 19, 72, 133, 139
Montgomery, Drew, 43
Montreal Olympics, 89–90, 115
Moore, Ann, 89
Morin, Regina Anne (Gina), 12–14
Morris, George, 3, 59, 61, 65, 67, 68, 69, 70, 82, 91, 133, 134, 136
Mud Dauber, 90

Munich Olympics, 57, 87–89, 118
Murphy, Dennis, 72, 92
Myles, Emily, 19

N

National Horse Show, 5, 40, 42, 43, 52, 57, 65, 69, 70, 71, 75, 132
Nations Cup, 31, 57, 63, 64, 72, 89, 92, 94
Nautical, 59, 60–61, 63, 67, 80–81
New York Herald Tribune, 67, 70
Night Owl, 59, 67, 69, 81

O

Oak Brook, 46, 97
O'Dwyer, Ged, 33
Olympic course, 101, 119
Olympic Games, 19, 23, 31, 42, 43, 44, 45, 47–53, 79, 90, 107, 115, 121, 139
  Helsinki, 63, 67
  Mexico, 65, 84–86, 116, 118
  Montreal, 89–90, 115
  Munich, 57, 87–89, 118
  Rome, 63, 64, 66, 68, 69, 70, 81–82
  Stockholm, 80–81
  Tokyo, 82, 84, 92, 118
  USET debut at, 46
Open Jumper course, 103
Open Jumpers, 113
Ox Ridge Hunt Club, 44, 118

P

Pacific Coast Hunter Seat Championship, 70
Pan American Games, 19, 36, 46, 52, 57, 65, 71, 72, 90–94, 97, 139
Passo Corese, 11
Plattny, Captain Joszef, 31
Preliminary course, 103
President's Cup, 72
Prince of Wales Cup, 69

194

INDEX

Prize of Nations, 46, 80, 89, 92
Professional Horseman's Association (PHA), 70
Psalm, 89
Puissance class, 40, 63, 69, 70, 136

Q

Queen Elizabeth II Cup, 57

R

Rails, importance of in course design, 99
Randolph, Mrs. A.C., 67
Rath, Patrick, 91
Ridland, Robert, 89
Reflector, 67
Reins, 17
Riding
   as a sport, 39
   building confidence, 10
   de Némethy's views on, 6, 7, 100
   "Gladstone" style of, 48
Riding and Schooling Horses, 14
Riviera Wonder, 66, 67, 70
Robert, Michel, 136
Rodenas, Paula, 114
Rolex Kentucky Trials, 132
Rome Olympics, 63, 64, 66, 68, 69, 70, 81–82
Royal International Horse Show, 57, 61, 63
Royal Winter Fair, Toronto, 71
Royce A. Drake Memorial Challenge Trophy, 66
Russell, John, 46, 80

S

Sandsablaze, 92
Sands Point Horse Show, 70
San Lucas, 59, 65, 71
Sansalve, 69
Saumer, 136
Schooling Your Horse, 15
School of Riding, de Némethy, 24
Sears, Eleanora, 36, 67

Secor Farms, 44
Senderos, Fernando, 93
Shady Lake, 71
Shapiro, Neal, 58, 70, 71, 87, 89
Show jumping, 37–43, 114
   and the USET, 43–46, 47–53
   course design, 40, 97–107
   future of, 136–142
   Olympics, 46, 52, 57
Side reins, 17
Silver City, 67
Silverminer, 67
Simonetti, Americo, 91
Sinbad, 67
Sinjon, 59, 69, 91
Sloopy, 58, 89
Smith, Cappy, 67
Smith, Melanie, 19, 72, 93, 106, 107, 138, 139
Smythe, Pat, 19
Snowbound, 59, 71, 72
Snow Man, 68, 70
Southern Pines, 46
Southern Squirrel, 67
Spanish Riding School of Vienna, 10
Stackpole, General Albert, 43
Staley, Walter, 90
Stecken, Fritz, 33
Steinkraus, William, 3, 23, 34, 46, 59, 61–72, 79–82, 85, 86, 87, 89, 90, 91, 92, 116, 120, 121, 139, 142
Stockholm Olympics, 80–81
Stone, Whitney, 43, 118
Stoneyhill Farm, 13, 24
Stroller, 138
Stuekelberger, Christine, 132

T

Tally Ho, 67, 69
Team Championship, 65
Tennessee Walkers, 44
Third Level dressage, 114
Thoroughbreds, 31, 67, 126, 137–138
Tokyo Olympics, 82, 84, 92, 118
Tomboy, 59, 71, 84, 91
Toytown, 67

195

INDEX

Trail Guide, 64, 67, 69, 80
Traurig, Bernie, 70
Tuckerman, General Alfred G., 43

U

Uncle Max, 70
Uncle Tom, 71
United States Equestrian Team (USET), 3, 36, 37, 42, 43–46, 97, 120, 121, 126, 138, 142
    de Némethy as coach of, 47–53, 57, 58, 59–76, 80–94, 97, 138
    major jumping victories, 145–190
    See also Olympic Games and Pan American Games
U.S. Jumping Team, 3
Untermyer, Alvin, 43, 44
Untouchable, 71
USET Book of Riding, 126

V

Valdes, Alberto, 90
Valko, Captain Charles, 31
Vanderbilt, Alfred Gwynne, 42
Venezuela equine encephamyelitis (VEE), 92
Venus de Ver, 136
Viscount, 65
von Visy, Stefan, 70

W

Washington International, 52, 57–58, 71
Weed, J. Spencer, 43
Westchester Pony Club, 19
Wheeler, John R., 91
White City Show, 69
White Lightening, 65
Whitney Stone Memorial Cup, 138
Wiley, Hugh, 59–63, 65, 67–70, 80, 82, 91, 133
Windsor Castle, 67, 70, 138
Winkler, Hans, 87
Winnett, John, 79
Wofford, Colonel John, 43
Wonabet, 67
World Championship, 5, 23, 57, 69, 139
World Cup, 5, 52, 75
    course, 100–103
Wright, Gordon, 14, 68

Z

Zeiler, Peter, 58